CHILDREN, FAMILY AND THE STATE

LIVE QUESTIONS IN ETHICS AND MORAL PHILOSOPHY

Tom Sorell, University of Essex, UK
Norman Bowie, University of Minnesota, USA, and London Business School, UK

The series offers short, accessible studies addressing some of the most topical questions shared by moral philosophy and the social sciences. Written by leading figures who have published extensively in the chosen area, single-author volumes in the series review the most recent literature and identify what the author thinks are the most promising approaches to the live questions selected. The authors are philosophers who appreciate the importance and relevance of empirical work in their area. In addition to single-author volumes, the series will include collections of contributions on live questions. The collections will consist of important published literature and freshly commissioned pieces, with introductions explaining why the contributions represent progress in the treatment of the live questions selected.

Children, Family and the State

DAVID WILLIAM ARCHARD

Routledge
Taylor & Francis Group
LONDON AND NEW YORK

First published 2003 by Ashgate Publishing

Reissued 2018 by Routledge
2 Park Square, Milton Park, Abingdon, Oxon OX14 4RN
711 Third Avenue, New York, NY 10017, USA

Routledge is an imprint of the Taylor & Francis Group, an informa business

A Library of Congress record exists under LC control number: 2002026235

ISBN 13: 978-1-138-71933-0 (hbk)
ISBN 13: 978-1-138-71927-9 (pbk)
ISBN 13: 978-1-315-19430-1 (ebk)

Contents

Preface

I am very grateful to Tom Sorrell for inviting me to write this book and for providing helpful comments on a first draft. I would also like to thank Hillel Steiner for clarifying, in correspondence, his understanding of rights.

This book was completed while I was a Visiting Fellow at the Centre of Applied Philosophy and Professional Ethics at the University of Melbourne. I am immensely grateful to the Centre for providing me with a tremendously congenial and stimulating atmosphere in which to work. I am particularly indebted to Tony Coady for his help while I was there.

As always, I am indebted to my partner, Bernarde, for her suggestions, criticisms and loving support of my writing.

As the book's 'Introduction' states, the question of how a society treats its children is a very practical one. Save the Children is the leading charity working nationally and internationally to create a better future for children. The book's royalties are being donated to this charity.

For the past few years I have been a member of the Dundee Children's Panel. The Scottish Children's Hearing System is a unique and, I believe, irreplaceable arrangement for dealing with children in trouble. I have learnt more than I can say about the problems children face in our society and about the ways in which we might deal with these problems by working within the system. In consequence, this book is dedicated to all my fellow panel members and to its reporters.

Introduction

This book, as its title suggests, has three parts. Each part – 'children', 'the family' and 'the state' – is the subject of a separate chapter. The first chapter concerns children. In particular, it asks if children have all, or even some, of the rights that adults have and, if they do not, what guarantees there can be that children will be treated in the morally appropriate ways. Two things that are nowadays considered to be guaranteed to children – by key principles in the relevant legislation and charters of human rights – are that their best interests are promoted and that their voice on matters affecting their interests are heard. Chapter 1 concludes by considering what these two principles might mean.

For the most part, children are brought up in families as seems to have been the case throughout history. Chapter 2 considers what a family is and specifically examines the rights of the adult members of families. Do adults have a right to found a family, and what might that mean? Do parents have rights over their children? Where do any of these rights derive from? The family is also a social institution that can be appraised in the light of the ideal of justice. The existence of families may serve or constrain the realization of social justice. They may do so in two ways. Families themselves may be just or unjust institutions, but there can also be justice, or injustice, between different families. Chapter 2 concludes by asking what justice demands of the family.

The third, and final, element in the story is the state – an independent party standing apart from parents and children. In this role it may seek to promote certain public ends; but it can also act as the representative of the child as well as the final arbitrator in disputes between the child and others. What is the proper balance between the interests of the child, the parent and the state? The final chapter tries to answer this question not in the abstract but by reference to three important social, legal and political areas in which these interests can contend namely – education, child protection and the medical treatment of children. Thus the chapter tries to answer such questions as 'Why should children be compulsorily educated?', 'What rights do parents have to determine the content of their child's education?', 'What principles guide child protection practice?', 'How can a state act to protect the interests of a child whilst respecting the integrity of the family?', 'Who decides what medically should happen to a child?' and 'Should children be required to provide medical assistance to others?'.

Although the kinds of topic dealt with and the sorts of question raised in each chapter are different there are clear interrelationships between the various parts of the book. Claims, arguments and principles introduced in Chapter 1 are revisited in later chapters so that, hopefully, a richer understanding is gained by setting them in the fuller context. Consider, for instance, the principle that a child's 'best interests' should be promoted. First we need to understand exactly what this means. For example, is it identical to what the child would choose for herself if she were an adult? We also need to be clear about what promoting the best interests of a child means for the adult who is the child's parent or guardian. Can one person (in this case, a parent) reasonably be asked to do the best for somebody else (her child)? What sense does it make to speak of parental rights if parents must promote the best interests of their child? Finally, it seems that the state has its own role to play in promoting the best interests of the child. How is this requirement to be balanced against the interests, and views, of both the parent and the child?

Asking these questions is both possible and necessary. It is possible because the last 30 years have seen a huge, and frequently commented upon, revival in substantive political and moral theory. This means that the resources exist to enable a rich and sophisticated understanding of key principles and leading concepts to be applied to the subject under consideration in this book. Thus, for instance, our grasp of what a right is or of what justice or equality of opportunity requires is that much greater than before.

Asking the questions instanced earlier is also a necessity. There is now a greater recognition that the moral and political status of children merits extended treatment. Feminist critics of the history of ideas often complain that women have been written out of the story: they simply do not make an appearance or are merely assimilated into the household whose head is male. Much the same sort of complaint can be made on behalf of children. Moral and political philosophers have had little to say about them. Of course philosophers in the past have written about children, the family and education (Turner and Matthews, 1998). Plato, Locke and Rousseau are perhaps the most prominent philosophers to have devoted attention to the question of how children should be brought up (Plato, 1941; Locke, 1960; Rousseau, 1991). Few, however, have written explicitly on the nature and significance of childhood. As for the family, a contemporary surveyor of work in political philosophy has observed that '[t]he family has not so much been relegated to the private sphere, as simply ignored entirely' (Kymlicka 2002: 398).

This judgement is perhaps a little unfair. During the last 20 years there has been a spate of work – the vast majority of it in the form of edited collections – devoted to philosophical considerations of the family, parenthood and the status of the child (O'Neill and Ruddick, 1979; Aiken and LaFollette 1980; Scarre, 1989; Alston *et al.*, 1992; Meyers *et al.*, 1993; Ulanowsky, 1995;

Ladd, 1996; Nelson, 1997; Houlgate, 1998; Archard and Macleod, 2002). There have been fewer monographs on the subject of children (Archard, 1993b; Blustein, 1982). It is also true that a contemporary encyclopedia of philosophy has no entry for 'children' or 'childhood', although one for 'ethics and the family' (Craig, 1998), that discussion of the family in a companion to ethics is subsumed under an entry on 'personal relationships' (LaFollette, 1993) and that children do not figure in a companion to contemporary political philosophy (Goodin and Pettit, 1993). The topic of children is most directly addressed in treatises on medical ethics where the issue of informed consent looms large.

The growing philosophical interest in childhood, children and the family can be attributed to at least four factors. First, there has been considerable interest in rights and in the key question of who may appropriately be thought of as rights-holders. Children represent an interesting 'test-case' for this latter question. Second, there has been growing attention to the topic of civic education and to the acquisition by adults of the skills, dispositions, virtues and knowledge necessary to function as citizens within a flourishing liberal democratic society. Children must, of course, become those adults. Third, the topic of justice figures large in contemporary moral and political philosophy, due, in considerable part, to the publication of Rawls, major treatise, *A Theory of Justice* (1972) which provoked the revival in normative theory. Further, Rawls himself considers that the existence of the family is an obstacle to the full realization of a liberal principle of fair opportunity and even asks – rhetorically it would seem – if the family ought to be abolished (Rawls, 1972: 74; 301, 511). This has promoted considerable discussion of the relationship between justice and family. Fourth, and finally, social and political philosophers cannot but strive to understand changes in their own society. In recent years we have witnessed the impact of the possibilities generated by the new reproductive technology. At the same time, but over a more protracted period, there have been continued significant changes in familial forms, including the rise of single parenthood, a steady increase in divorce rates, greater numbers of women at work and the recognition, socially and legally, of single sex unions.

Seeking to answer the philosophical questions raised above is not merely a theoretical matter. How we treat our children – how we rear and educate them, punish them for their crimes, what social and political status we accord them, how we seek to protect them by our laws and policies – is a profoundly revealing index of our society's character. No society is more condemned than one that abandons its young to abuse, neglect and cruelty. No society is more highly esteemed than one that cherishes its young and promotes their interests. We cannot, moreover, remain indifferent to the fact that broader social and economic inequalities – both within and between societies – are reflected in the condition of children. Within rich developed nations thousands of children will endure poverty, bad housing, reduced educational opportunities, low standards of health care, and malnutrition or poor diet. In the world at large, millions of children are denied even a basic education, and die from starvation or from curable diseases.

This book is a guide to some of the most important lines of thought about the child, the family and the state in social, moral and political philosophy. It is written as an introductory academic text. However, although the book does not continually attend to the practical context no one should be in any doubt that theorizing about its topic has a point and applicability in the real world we share with children.

Chapter 1

Children

Children are young human beings. Some children are very young human beings. As human beings, children evidently have a certain moral status. There are things that should not be done to them and should not be done to them for the simple reason that they are human. At the same time, children are different from adult human beings and it seems reasonable to think that there are things children may not do that adults are permitted to do. We do not, after all and as a matter of law, allow children to vote, to marry, to buy alcohol, to have sex or to engage in paid employment. What makes children a special case for philosophical consideration is this combination of their humanity and their youth, or, more exactly, what is thought to be associated with their youth.

Children and Rights

One very obvious way in which the question of what children are entitled to do or to be or to have is raised by asking whether children have rights. If so, do they have all the rights that adults have and do they have rights that adults do not have? If they do not have rights how do we ensure that they are treated in the morally right way? Children certainly have rights under law in most jurisdictions. There is also the United Nations Convention on the Rights of the Child adopted in 1980 and ratified within a year by 20 countries. This Convention accords to children a wide range of rights including the right to freedom of expression (Article 13), the right to freedom of thought, conscience and religion (Article 14), the right to freedom of association (Article 15), the right to 'a standard of living adequate for the child's physical, mental, spiritual, moral and social development' (Article 27) and the right to education (Article 28).

Law – in the form of a statute or a constitution or a convention – may accord 'positive' rights to children, as it may do to any stipulated category of legal rights-holders. However, it is normal to distinguish between 'positive' rights – those that are recognized in law – and 'moral' rights – those that are recognized by some moral theory. That children have 'positive' rights does not, then, settle the question of whether they do, or should have, moral rights.

Incidentally, Article 1 of the United Nations Convention defines a child as any human being below the age of 18 years 'unless', it adds, 'under the law applicable to the child, majority is attained earlier' (United Nations, 1989). In what follows this definition will be assumed. Of course, we may need, in some context, to draw attention to the notable differences that do exist between the very young – that is, infants – and older teenagers. But, unless otherwise indicated, a child is simply a young person who has not reached the age that the law and social convention determines as her majority. There are, of course, important questions as to how we define childhood and as to how we think about childhood as a special stage of human development. I have treated these questions elsewhere (Archard, 1993b: Ch. 2). In this book I shall ignore these questions and concentrate instead on how children – given that we already know who they are – should be treated.

Some think it obvious that children do have rights and believe that the only interesting question is whether children possess all and only those rights which adults possess. Others are sceptical, believing that, given the nature both of rights and of children, it is wrong to think of children as rights-holders. One background worry against which such scepticism may be set is a currently oft-expressed concern at the proliferation of rights. Rights are, so it is alleged, now promiscuously ascribed in two ways. First, the list of rights-holders has been extensively lengthened. Second, many more demands are expressed as rights claims.

Of course, the worry is ill-founded if it is a concern simply and solely about numbers. Perhaps, defenders of extending rights will urge, this is a case where you cannot have too much of a good thing. No one should object to the addition of a bona fide right just because it is adding one more right to the list. However, the concern is more properly understood as the worry that the prodigality of rights attributions is damaging to the cause of rights. If you give away too many rights they may cease to have the value and significance they once had, and ought still to have. A favoured metaphor in this context is monetary: the inflation of rights talk devalues the currency of rights. That currency is indeed precious for it is almost universally accepted that rights, if they exist, are things whose possession is of advantage to those who possess them. Indeed, on some accounts of rights their possession is of very great advantage to their owners. It should disquiet those who seek to increase the number of such a good thing that it might cease to be so good a thing if it is too liberally distributed.

This thought must caution the defenders of children's rights since, after all, talk of children having rights has post-dated the introduction and general acceptance of rights talk as such. There are, however, more particular reasons for being suspicious of the idea that children have rights, and, to appreciate these, it is necessary to be clearer about the language of rights. With respect to rights in general we can inquire as to what it is to have a right, or, put another way, what being a rights-holder consists in. As we shall see, there are here two competing accounts, one of which is seen as fatal to the idea of children as rights-holders. We can also ask a different question – namely, what must be true for there to be rights. That is, we can try to specify what have been called the 'existence conditions for rights' (Sumner, 1987: 10–11). We can also construct a taxonomy of the different kinds of right. Finally, we can ask what the moral significance of having a right is, or what weight rights have. Some, for instance, have viewed rights as being absolute such that the fact of a person's possession of a right is sufficient to outweigh or discount all other moral considerations (Nozick, 1974). Others believe the possession of rights to be a weighty consideration but not so weighty as to outbalance every other moral claim. With regard to any acknowledged right we can identify it by means of its content (what is it a right to?) and its scope (who has it and against whom do they have it?), as well as its weight relative to other rights and to other moral considerations. Some believe that rights never conflict. But, if they do, we need to know which right should have priority. Not all of these questions are relevant when we want to focus on the particular issue of whether or not children have rights, and, if so, which ones. However the first question raised above is especially salient.

Theories of Rights

So what is it to have a right? Here, there are two competing theories whose respective virtues and vices have been extensively debated without either gaining evident or agreed supremacy. In one camp is the will or choice theory (Hart, 1973; Sumner, 1987; Steiner, 1994); in the opposing camp is the welfare or interest theory (MacCormick, 1982; Raz, 1984; Kramer, 1998). The will or choice theory sees a right as the protected exercise of choice. In particular, to have a right is to have the power to enforce or waive the duty of which the right is the correlative. On this theory, what it means for me to have the right to education is for me to have the option of enforcing the duty of some other person or persons to provide me with an education, or to discharge them from the responsibility of doing so. The welfare or interest theory sees a right as the protection of an interest of sufficient importance to impose on others certain duties whose discharge allows the right-holder to enjoy the interest in question. Here, what it means for me to have a right to education is for me to have an interest in being educated which is so important that others are under an enforceable duty to provide me with an education.

Each of the above theories is alleged to have failings but, interestingly, in this present context one defect of the will theory – so its critics argue – is its exclusion of some human beings from the category of rights-holders. This is because whilst all human beings, and perhaps many classes of non-human beings such as animals, have interests that ought to be protected, not all human beings have the capacity to exercise choice. Children – along with the severely mentally disabled and the comatose – cannot thus, on the will theory, be the holders of rights. For at least one prominent defender of the interest theory the fact that children evidently do have rights is sufficient to display the falsity of the will theory, thus making children a 'test-case' for the latter (MacCormick, 1982). Of course, someone who is convinced of the correctness of the will theory might readily concede that the theory entails the denial of rights to children but see no reason to abandon the theory. For her the entailment is not 'Children have rights. Therefore, the will theory is false'. It is 'The will theory is true. Therefore, children cannot have rights'.

To help our understanding of the complex issues at stake I will set out the different claims, some of them competing, in a way that shows the role they play in various possible arguments:

1 Rights are protected choices.
2 Only those capable of exercising choices can be rights-holders.
3 Children are incapable of exercising choice.
4 Children are not rights-holders.
5 Adults have duties to protect the important interests of children.
6 Rights and duties are correlative.
7 Children are rights-holders.

Let me explain (6). An important claim held by many is that for each and every right there is a correlative duty. To say that I have a right to something is just to say that someone else has a duty to me in respect of that thing. Rights and duties are, as it were, simply the two sides of one and the same single coin. Some duties do not correlate with rights. But for each and every right there is a correlative, and enforceable duty. Now, clearly, (4) and (7) contradict one another: either children are rights-holders or they are not. But (4) follows from (2) and (3), which are consequences of the will theory. On the other hand, (7) follows from (5) and (6) which give expression to the interest theory. It does so only if the duties adults have to children are such that they correlate with rights. So, as things stand, either the will theory is true and children do not have rights, or the interest theory is true and they do. Or, put another way, either children have rights in which case the will theory cannot be true, or they do not in which case that theory could be true.

How might the various protagonists in these debates respond to these different claims? A will theorist who did not want to deny that children have rights might deny (2). He might say that although it is true that children are themselves incapable of exercising choice, it does not follow that they cannot still be possessors of rights. For children might have representatives, such as most obviously their parents or guardians, who could exercise the choices on their behalf. The representatives would choose for the children as the children would choose if they were capable of choosing for themselves. This proxy exercise of choice would take place only during the period when the children were incapable of exercising choice and in acknowledgement of the fact that the children will eventually be capable of exercising their own choices. In short, children still have rights but the choices, which are constitutive of these rights according to the will theory, are made by representatives of the children. The will theory's most prominent defender (Hart, 1973: 184 n. 86) makes just such a modification of the will theory in respect of children.

Now, such a modification must meet a number of challenges. First, how should the representatives be selected? Should those empowered to act as representatives be those who are most likely to choose as the children would choose if capable, or are there are other independent grounds on which they are selected, such as, most obviously, that they are the child's parents? We might think of the representation of the children as an entrusting to the representatives, the trustees, of the choices of the truster, the child. Now, second, are the terms of the trust sufficiently clear and determinate? Is it, for instance, perspicuous and evident what a child would choose if capable of choosing? Note that the criterion is not what is in the best interests of the child for, consistent with the will theory, we must appeal to choices rather than interests. It is not easy to say what some adult who cannot currently choose – because she is, for instance, temporarily comatose – would choose if able. It is even harder in the case of someone, a child, who is for the period of childhood simply incapable of making any choices. Indeed, this is a problem that I will examine in much greater detail later in this chapter when I consider 'best interests' in terms of hypothetical or substituted choice. Third, how is the trust to be enforced and by whom? The representative may be presumed to have a duty to choose as the child would choose if able. If rights are correlative with duties then someone other than the representative and the child must be in a position to enforce or waive this duty. Could this be the state or its representative?

These are formidable challenges but, assuming they can be met, it is within the resources of the will theory to accord rights to children. That is significant for it means that children are not a straightforward 'test-case' for determining which theory of rights is correct. There are, moreover, two further responses that can be made by the will theorist to the claims listed earlier that challenge the presuppositions of the interest theory. First, she might accept (6) – that rights and duties are correlative – but deny or at least significantly modify (5) – that adults have duties to protect the important interests of children. She could say that the duties that are rightly specified under (5) are not the duties that correlate with rights. This is just to say, as all rights theorists will repeatedly say, that rights do not exhaust the moral domain. What we must do because others have rights against us is not everything we must morally do. There are duties beyond those rights-correlated duties. Consequently, we should, as adults, ensure that the interests of children are protected and promoted. It does not follow that they have rights against us. Likewise, we should not cruelly and gratuitously maltreat animals, but we need not think that it follows from this that animals are rights-holders.

Second, a will theorist might accept (5) and (6) as they stand but say that the rights which correlate with these duties are possessed not by the children but by adults who are in the best position to protect the children. Indeed, they might press home their point by asking whether it really matters whether the rights are held by the children or by those who would act as best they could for the children (Steiner, 1998: 261).

This review of the will and interest theory has not

considered other reasons – independent of the implications of either theory for the question of whether or not children have rights – for favouring either theory. It has simply examined the issue of whether the denial of children's rights can be thought of as a test case for the probity of the will theory. Of course, even if it is not such a test case there may be other considerations that tell against the will theory and in favour of the interest theory. Or it may be that, on balance, the interest theory is preferable to the will theory whether or not the latter denies rights to children.

Children's Rights?

I will leave these debates to one side. Let me grant that, on either account of what it is to have a right, children could, in principle, be the holders of rights. If this still seems highly unlikely in the case of will theory, then let it be assumed that the interest theory is correct. This assumption is made only so that we can address the further questions. Ought children to have rights? And, if so, what rights should they have?

Should children have rights? There are those who claim that children should have all the rights that adults presently have. They are known as 'liberationists' and include Holt, Farson and Cohen (Farson 1974; Holt 1975; Cohen, H., 1980). We can distinguish real from rhetorical liberationists. The latter are those who see the demand for equal rights for children as a means both of drawing attention to the discrimination that children suffer by comparison with adults in their treatment and in improving their condition. A rhetorical liberationist does not actually believe that children should be the equals of adults. Rather, he thinks that claiming as much is the best way of advancing their interests. By contrast, a real liberationist does view children as the equals of adults. Their case will be considered in due course. In addition, there are those who think that children should have some, but not all, of the rights which adults have. A common view is that children should not have liberty rights (rights to choose, such as to vote, practise a religion and to associate) but should at least have welfare rights (rights that protect important interests, such as health). The various possibilities within this view will be further considered in due course.

Finally, there are those who think that children should not have any rights. Or, put less brusquely, they are sceptical, for theoretical and political reasons, about attributing rights to children. Their case, which I will examine first, is made in three ways. The first is to assert what liberationists deny – namely, that children are not qualified, as adults are, to have rights. The second is to argue that the ascription of rights to children is inappropriate because it displays a misunderstanding of what childhood is, what children are like, or what relationships children stand in to adults. The third is to argue that, notwithstanding their lack of rights, children can be assured of adequate moral protection by other means.

Let me take the first claim first. The question of qualification is the question of whether children have the requisite *capacity* for rights. We have already seen that, on the will theory of rights, the capacity to exercise choice is a necessary condition of having a right. Since, arguably, children lack such a capacity they cannot, on the will theory at least, possess rights. There is a more general issue of capacity that is in dispute whatever theory of rights is defended and that follows from attention to the matter of what it is that rights do. Rights have a content – that is, each right is a right to do, to be or to have something. Rights also have a certain weight – that is, they function, morally or legally, to protect and to promote whatever it is that the right is a right to by allowing for the enforcement of the correlate duties. For instance, a right to health care imposes on others an enforceable duty to provide the right-holder with the means by which her health may be safeguarded. A right to vote obligates others to allow the right-holder to cast her vote, if and as she chooses, in regular elections.

Such rights are important to those who hold them because what it is that they protect and promote matters to them. At a minimum, then, a rights-holder should be somebody for whom what the right protects matters. It seems evident, to take a simple example, that a very young child has no interest in marrying, and thus that a right to marry is inappropriately attributed to such a child. It might be countered that a very young child does have an interest in *not* marrying on account of what that might mean for her. It may well be true that, irrespective of what a very young child is interested in, she has an interest in not being married. However, this is not an interest of which the very young child can appreciate or understand the significance. Moreover it remains the case that she is neither interested in, nor can she be said to have an interest in, entering the state of marriage.

At this stage we can make use of the distinction between 'welfare' and 'liberty' rights, which is independent of that between interest and choice. The latter distinction marks a difference between opposing theories of what it is to have a right, whereas the distinction between 'welfare' and 'liberty' is one between the content of rights. Liberty rights are rights to choose, such as whether and for whom to vote; welfare rights are rights to the protection of fundamental aspects of one's welfare, such as one's physical and mental health.

Children lack certain cognitive abilities – for example, to acquire and to process information in an ordered fashion, to form consistent and stable beliefs, and to appreciate the significance of options and their consequences. They also lack certain volitional abilities – for example, to form, retain and act in the light of consistent desires, and to make independent choices. Children are not unique amongst human beings in this respect; adults who are seriously mentally impaired are also disqualified in this sense – which simply means, of course, these adults are childlike. However, children are unique in that not all human beings are seriously mentally impaired, but all human beings were once children. Thus every one of us was, during our early years, not qualified to be a rights-holder even if now we are so qualified.

A child's incapacity, in the sense indicated above, disqualifies them from having liberty rights. Someone incapable of choosing cannot have a right whose content is a fundamental choice. But surely children are human beings whose welfare matters? Indeed they are. However it is a moot point whether they are beings whose welfare matters *to them*. That is, they may, in virtue of the incapacity which disqualifies them from having liberty rights, be unable to understand what it is to be better or worse off, why that is significant, and what needs to be done or not done to make a difference in this regard.

In other words, it is arguable that rights-holders should be able to grasp the importance of the content of rights that they should know, for instance, the significance of being healthy and of voting. Further, rights-holders should be able to understand how a right functions in protecting the content of the right. The capacity in question is an ability to make sense of one's life and what is of value within it. There is no point in giving rights to those who cannot see what rights are or do. Such, runs the argument of those who would deny rights to children, is the case with the young. They lack the requisite capacity for rights. They lack the capacity to make choices and should not have liberty rights. They lack the capacity to understand what is in their interests and should not have welfare rights.

I will say more about the question of capacity when I examine the liberationist case. But let me turn now to the second claim that may be made in denying rights to children – namely, that the ascription of rights to children is inappropriate because it displays a misunderstanding of what childhood is, of what children are like, or of what relationships children do or ought to stand in to adults. This claim comes in various forms. Let me cite and discuss some of them.

Onora O'Neill (1988) believes that we should start our thinking about what morally we owe to children by specifying our obligations as adults to them. There certainly exist what are called *perfect* obligations – obligations that are either owed to all children or to some specified set of children. They are perfect in that it is completely specified whom they are owed to and what is owed to them. We all are obliged not to maltreat any child, and parents have a particular duty to care for *their* children. But there are also *imperfect* obligations, which are those of caring for children to whom we do not, as parents for instance, have specific obligations. All adults owe these but they are not owed to all children (how could they possibly be?) nor is it specified what precisely is owed to them (this will depend on circumstances).

Perhaps, then, we can agree that we are all under a duty to prevent the abuse of children. But clearly we cannot, as individuals, each act to stop every child being abused. Moreover what we ought to do – for instance, by reporting suspected cases of abuse – will depend on the circumstances and also on what is in place by way of particular institutions and laws to deal with child abuse.

Crucially, whilst perfect obligations correlate with rights, imperfect obligations do not. This means that anyone who starts and finishes thinking about what is morally owed to children in terms of their rights is unable to capture what imperfect obligations express. Yet this is to miss much of what is most important about the way in which, morally, we should as adults stand in relation to children, for the fulfilment of these imperfect duties of care and concern is what centrally protects and promotes the lives of children as children. Thinking ethically about children's lives in terms of their putative rights is to misperceive what is of central importance and value in these lives.

A response to O'Neill's argument is given by Coady (1992). She does not deny that perfect obligations correlate with rights. Thus to the extent that we do have perfect obligations to children they do have corresponding rights. Yet O'Neill denies that imperfect obligations correlate with rights. But why should we think that? The imperfect obligations are fundamental ones. They are not supererogatory – that is, beyond duty. Adults *must* show consideration and kindness to children in general. So why cannot children claim such kindness and consideration from adults as their right? O'Neill does say that when imperfect obligations are institutionalized – when, for instance, there are laws and institutions specifying who should act and how to detect and prevent child abuse – there are created positive special obligations to which correspond positive rights. But she adds that the obligations of, say, the social worker exceed the positive obligations associated with her job. However, this is true of all our obligations, whether perfect or imperfect. A parent can have positive – that is, legally recognized and sanctioned – duties to her child; she may, for instance, have no choice but to send her child to school. Yet her perfect obligations to her children are not exhaustively specified by what the law requires of her.

O'Neill's argument does not rely on any specification of the content of the obligations that might be owed by adults to children. Rather it is about the structure of our moral reasoning in respect of children, and the priority – false in the argument's view – that is given to rights. As an argument it thus bears some comparison with a view that expresses general scepticism about rights in the context of adult–child relations and which emphasizes the particular character of the family (Schrag, 1980; Schoeman, 1980). This view draws attention to the quality and nature of the relationships within a family, which are marked by a special intimacy and by deep, unconditional love between its members. One can grant that many families do not conform to this ideal and yet acknowledge that the family which does conform to it is a distinctive, and distinctively valuable, form of human association.

What arguably follows from this ideal of the family is the inappropriateness of asserting or claiming rights, for to do so would be to subvert and ultimately destroy what constitutes the family as the distinctive form of human association it is. Appeal is being made here to a familiar and oft-drawn distinction between two ways in which individuals engaged in a common enterprise or bound together in some enduring association can be assured of their beneficent, or at least minimally good, treatment of one another. One way is by the recognition – in law or custom or shared morality – of rights that all individuals can claim, or by rules of justice – similarly and generally recognized – which provide an assurance of fair treatment. Another way is by reliance on the dispositions or attitudes that the individuals bound together have, spontaneously and naturally, towards one another. Thus, for instance, if all are motivated by general benevolence in respect of all, no one has any need to claim or assert what is due to him as of right or rule. In the case of the family, it is argued, neither justice nor benevolence suffices, but love does.

A further and quite distinct allegation is that not only is there no need for any such claims, but that allowing them to be made will erode, and in due course destroy, the dispositions and attitudes that rendered the need for rights and rules of justices unnecessary in the first place. This further claim is an influential one in the general critique communitarianism makes, within political philosophy, of what is characterized as a rights-based and individualistic liberalism (see, for instance, Sandel, 1982: 32–35). In the context of the family, the claim is that granting its members rights will subvert and bring about the end of the love between them that made rights superfluous. These claims will be further discussed in Chapter 2 since they touch crucially on the issue of intra-familial justice.

The arguments thus far have appealed to the role that rights generally do, and should, play in our moral lives. A further argument considers what would actually follow from granting rights to children (Purdy, 1992). The argument is that, as adults, we need to have acquired certain traits of character if we are to be able to pursue our goals and lead a valuable life. To acquire these traits it is essential that we not be allowed, as children, to make our own choices. Granting children the liberty to exercise rights is destructive of the preconditions for the possibility of having fulfilling adult lives. The central, and empirical, premise in this argument is that children do not spontaneously and naturally grow into adults. They need to be nurtured, supported and, more particularly, subjected to control and discipline. Without that context, giving children the rights that adults have is not only bad for the children but is also bad for the adults they will turn into, and for the society we share as adults and children.

The defence of the view that children should not, as the liberationist asserts, have all the rights that adults have has involved the following assertions. First, children simply lack the capacities that qualify adults for the possession of rights. Second, talk of children's rights does not capture the truth about their lives or about the family, or encourages destructive permissiveness that has poor consequences for adults and their society. Third, such a denial of a rights is not bad for children.

One can thus maintain, as we saw earlier when discussing the will and interest theories of rights, that rights do not exhaust the moral domain. There are things we ought to do which do not correspond to the obligations we have as correlates of rights. As adults, we should protect and promote the welfare of children, but it need not follow that they have rights against us. To repeat, humans should not wantonly maltreat animals, but we can insist on this without giving animals rights.

But does not talk of the rights of children nevertheless still serve a political or rhetorical function by reminding of us of what must be done for them? Might not such talk also serve as a critique of the extent to which we, as adults, may maintain children in an artificial condition of dependence and vulnerability, denying them the opportunity to make their own choices? Are not children one of the last social groups to be emancipated as others, such as women and blacks, have already been, and is not the language of rights the appropriate mode in which to campaign for that emancipation? The reply (O'Neill, 1988: 459–63) is that such talk about rights misses what is distinctively different about children as a group – namely, that childhood is not a permanently maintained status associated with oppression or discrimination but, rather, a stage of human development which everyone goes through. Moreover, the adults who deny that children do have rights may nevertheless also believe that it is their duty to ensure that the children for whom they care do pass from childhood into adulthood.

Liberationism

The first claim in the defence of the denial of rights to children is that children are disqualified by virtue of their incapacity to have rights. This is precisely what the liberationists dissent from. Liberationists can allow that the key to the appropriateness of giving or not giving rights to children turns on capacity (Cohen, H., 1980: ix), but will nevertheless argue that children are not disqualified from having rights by virtue of their lack of a capacity possessed by adults. Let me distinguish two respects in which this liberationist case might be modified or qualified. The first is in its scope. The liberationist might claim that *all* children are qualified to have rights, or she might claim only that *some* children are so qualified. The latter is the more plausible position in view of the fact that the very young infant is evidently incapacitated. Indeed, some liberationists seem to recognize as much even whilst they insist that *every* child should have rights (Farson, 1974: 31, 172, 185). If the scope of the liberationist claim is thus limited, it does not amount to the view that no line dividing human rights-holders from human beings who lack rights should be drawn, but, rather, that such a line has been drawn in the wrong place.

A second possible qualification of the liberationist view is that giving rights to children will play an important part in their acquiring the qualifying capacity. It is not thus that children are capable now but illegitimately denied their rights but, rather, that they will only – or at least more readily or at an earlier stage – acquire that capacity if given their rights. The denial of rights to children is, on this account, one significant element in a culture that serves artificially to maintain children in their childlike state of dependence, vulnerability and immaturity. While conceding that children of a very young age are not sufficiently capable to have rights, and will not acquire that capacity even if given rights, this qualification insists that the denial of rights to children of a certain age on account of their alleged incapacity is simply self-confirming: they cannot have rights because they are incapable, but they are incapable only because they do not have these rights.

One plausible version of the claim refers to the facts of experience. Children, or at least children of a certain age, may not differ markedly from adults in respect of their cognitive and volitional capacities. They may be as capable as older humans of making their own minds up about what to do and be as independent in their resolution to act on their choices, but they may simply not have had as much experience of the world as their adult counterparts. Being thus naïve and inexperienced in the ways of the world they will not be as able – that is, as qualified – as older (and wiser) human beings are to make sensible choices. Granted such a lack of experience can be attributed to a lack of opportunities to exercise choice. If such a lack of opportunity is in turn attributable not simply to not having been around for as long but to a denial of the freedom to make their own choices, then there is a powerful case for liberty rights being extended, even if cautiously, to these young people.

There are different ways in which the liberationist claim about capacity – whether qualified or not – can be made. One is by defending a 'thin' definition of capacity. For example, it may be said that children can make choices if what this means is expressing preferences. A child who says she wants *x* thereby chooses *x*. Of course, the response is that the ability to choose, thus minimally defined, is indeed possessed by children (even fairly young children) but it is not a capacity sufficient to qualify for rights ownership. What is needed for that is more than simply the ability to express or communicate a desire; it is an ability to understand and appreciate the significance of the options facing one, together with independence of choice. After all, the animal who moves from one feeding bowl to another may be said thereby to 'choose' the food in the latter bowl. But the animal does not have a general capacity of choice sufficient to qualify it as a holder of liberty rights.

Arbitrariness

Liberationists might move in the other direction and argue that the capacity which qualifies adults to have rights is in fact not a capacity that most, or perhaps any, adults actually possess. Thus it will be said that no adult fully understands the nature of the choices she faces, nor is she consistent in her beliefs and desires, nor is she really independent of the influences of her environment and peers. Whether the liberationist urges a 'thin' definition of capacity – which the child satisfies as much as the adult – or argues that, on a 'thick' definition of capacity, neither adult nor child qualifies as capable, the point is the same: the alleged differences between children and adult in respect of a qualifying capacity are not sufficient to warrant the ascription of rights to the latter and their denial to the former.

This, then, is one way in which the charge that '*[a]ny* line which uses age to distinguish people with rights from people without can be shown to be arbitrary' (Cohen, H., 1980: 48) can be made. The line is arbitrary because, as a matter of fact, it does not mark a real division between capacities. However, there is another way in which the charge is made. This turns on the idea that dividing lines *as such* – '*any*' lines – are arbitrary. Let me explore this idea more formally. There is a class, C, of individuals who can be ranked in some agreed, objective manner. Within that ranking there is a threshold, T, which operates so that those individuals who fall above it, but not those below it, qualify for some good or benefit, G. Thus, by way of example, some professions or occupations, such as the police or army, may stipulate a certain minimum height requirement. Let it be 5 feet 6 inches. Now for all those, C, seeking entry into the profession five and a half feet marks the threshold, T, for entry into that profession and its possible rewards, G. Height can be objectively determined so that individuals can be subject to an agreed ranking. Note that the ranking is not just ordinal (Jones is taller than Smith who in turn is taller than Brown) but is also fixed by a cardinal measurement of height (Jones is 6 feet, Smith is 5 feet 6 inches, Brown is 5 feet 4 inches). Thus no one disputes that Brown is 5 feet 4 inches whereas Jones is 6 feet and Smith is 5 feet 6 inches, but one source of complaint will be the alleged arbitrariness of fixing on 5 feet 6 inches as T.

This complaint can have two distinguishable elements. One is an objection to the use of *any* height as T; the other is an objection to the use of *this* height as T. Now, of course, the reply to the first objection is that it is not so much height as such which matters but rather height as an index of the degree of physical presence or strength necessary to discharge the requirements of the job in question. The reply to the second objection is that this height is at least as good if not better than any other T in supplying a reliable indicator of the requisite physical attributes.

Height is an interesting example. Some argue that the use of height qualifications in professions such as the army, police and fire services have served to discriminate against female entrants into these jobs. Women in general are more unlikely than men in general to come up, literally, to the mark. Of course, if being a certain height *is* a reliable indication of one's ability to perform the job, then so much the worse for those – men and women – who fall below it. If more women than men fall below the specified threshold height, then that shows only that women are, in general, less equipped than men in general to perform their job. However, it would be a valid criticism of a particular height qualification that it was set too high and thus unfairly excluded disproportionately more women than men. The same would also apply if height is not a reliable indicator of one's ability to do a certain job that men in general and women in general are in fact equally well equipped to do.

How does this relate to age and rights? Again, the use of an age of majority – let us say 18 – as the T at which rights are secured will be objected to on two grounds. Either it will be said that the use of *any* age is arbitrary, or it will be said that the use of *this* age is arbitrary. The general reply to the first objection is that age as such is not the issue but rather the reliable correlation of age with the acquisition of those capacities that qualify a person for the attribution of rights. The second objection assumes that there is *some* age at which these capacities are acquired, but maintains that it is not 18. We have already seen that some liberationists might qualify their claim in respect of scope. That is, they do not dispute that there should be a T of age, but they do think that the conventional or orthodox T is fixed too late. We have also seen that liberationists may simply deny that there should be any T on the grounds that there just is no difference between children and adults in respect of their respective capacities for any T to mark. This version of the arbitrariness claim concedes that, if age functions as a T, it does so only inasmuch as it correlates with the acquisition of capacities which it is agreed are necessary qualifications for the possession of rights. In sum, the arbitrariness claim amounts either to the denial that the acquisition of the specified capacities does correlate with the T in question or to the denial that there is any age at which the capacities are acquired.

Setting aside this version of the arbitrariness claim what remains of the charge that '*[a]ny* line which uses age to distinguish people with rights from people without can be shown to be arbitrary'? There are two ideas. The first is that, whereas T serves to mark a difference within C, it is membership of C as such which is important. Or, relatedly, what is being distributed, G, is so important that all members of C should receive it. In the context of children and rights it is being human which should make the difference, not being of a certain age. On this view rights are too important to be denied or given to some human beings on account of their age.

The reply is simple. Being human does matter and it is precisely because they are human beings, albeit young ones, that children are entitled to be treated in ways that non-humans, such as animals, are not. However, it is rights that are being distributed and, to that end, T *does* mark a significant point. Although having rights is better than not having them, those who lack rights do not lack any moral status whatever. T marks an important division between subclasses of the general class. Both this division and the membership of the general class are properly acknowledged. Children are acknowledged to be human beings and yet to be young human beings.

The second idea is this. T does not mark a significant *enough* difference. This is a point about thresholds and marginal differences. Grant that there is a significant difference between receipt of G and lacking it, between having and not having rights. That difference is not proportionate to what lies immediately either side of T. Although there is a large difference between T + x and T – y when x and y are very large numbers there is no appreciable difference between them when x and y are small numbers. A 40-year-old differs greatly from a 4-year-old. Someone aged 18 years and 1 month does not differ greatly from someone aged 17 years and 11 months. While it is understandable that the 40-year-old should have rights whereas the 4-year-old should not, this is not the case for the latter pairing.

To repeat, this is a point about liminal differences – about the extent to which real differences between classes are displayed by the members situated at the edge of each class. For example, there is a large difference in law between being a drunk driver and being a sober driver, but there is not a large difference between having x and having x – 1 milligrams of alcohol in the blood. Nevertheless, some determinate volume of alcohol, such as x, is going to be taken as the threshold, T, of being drunk for the purposes of the law on drink driving.

The reply to this line of argument is as follows. It is conceded that there is a difference between the classes that T divides – between being a drunk driver and a sober driver in law, and between being too young to have rights and old enough to have them. *These* differences are *not* arbitrary. They are real and they are relevant to the question of whether G should be distributed, whether someone should or should not have rights, or whether someone should or should not be prosecuted for drink driving. Given that these differences need to be acknowledged, a threshold needs to be fixed. The fact that there are not significant – or significant enough – differences being distinguished between members at the edges of the two classes is the price paid for having to operate with a threshold.

But *is* this price one that has to be paid? Why should we not take each individual on her own and determine whether or not she is qualified for receipt of the good or burden in question? If we are concerned to prevent drink driving because it imperils other road users why shouldn't the police forces test the capacity of a driver to drive safely rather than a simple level of alcohol? If we think that a certain set of capacities qualifies a human being for possession of rights why do we not simply test each human being to see if she does indeed qualify by having the capacities in question? A threshold of age could be used, but it would be employed only as a rough indicator of the appropriate time at which the test might be conducted rather than as a substitute for the test. So, one might assume that a child of 16 is approaching the point at which she will be competent to possess rights and test her accordingly at that age. Failure to pass the test at 16 would not preclude her being re-examined at later times.

After all, it will be pressed, we do not think that someone who has had a certain number of driving lessons is thereby qualified to drive. On the whole, however, someone who has had more lessons is likely to be more qualified, and, after a certain number of lessons, a learner driver is in a position to submit herself for an examination of her ability to drive. However, it is the test that determines her aptitude to drive, not the extent of her pre-test learning. Why should it be any different with the acquisition of rights?

The problems with the suggested use of a test are various. First, there is the sheer administrative scale of its employment in such a case as human rights. Imagine what would be involved in testing each and every person to determine if they are qualified to have rights. Second, there is the problem of agreeing a determinate procedure for testing. How exactly are we to examine someone in respect of their competence to possess rights? It is, by comparison, a fairly simple matter to agree what shall count as a competence to drive and to test accordingly. Third, there is the problem of fairness. Any test must not unfairly disqualify some group of putative rights-holders by, for instance, having a bias in the testing procedure which, in effect, discriminates against that group. By way of comparison it has been alleged that some versions of intelligence testing – which are then used for the purposes of educational selection – are unfairly biased against ethnic groups and young girls. Consider, by contrast, how age as a threshold cannot be subject to any such bias. Everyone who matures reaches a particular age. Fourth, the administration of any official test – and especially one whose passing yields such important goods – is subject to the risks of corruption or of misuse for the self-interested ends of those administering it. Again, this cannot be true of the use of age as a threshold.

To summarize. The problems attaching to the use of a test are large and insuperable. The charges of arbitrariness have been shown to be false or overstated. Children do differ from adults in respect of their competence to possess rights. An age threshold is the appropriate way of registering that difference. One should, thus, acquire rights only on reaching a certain age. However, two riders to this summary are appropriate.

First, there is nothing wrong with the idea that different rights should be acquired at different ages. After all, it is plausible to think that the capacities needed for, and qualifying a person to possess, different rights are themselves different. More particularly, different rights would seem to require different degrees of competence. Liberty rights entitle their possessors to make choices, and the matters in respect of which choices are made differ in their complexity, importance and consequential impact. Those who are allowed to choose require greater or lesser amounts of maturity, independence and deliberative proficiency in order to be able to make these different kinds of choice. The decisions to marry, consume alcohol, serve in the armed forces, undertake paid labour, vote, buy goods in a shop, travel unaccompanied and open a bank account seem to presuppose different levels of understanding and autonomy. Assuming that these levels are progressively acquired at different ages it makes sense to accord the corresponding rights not all at once, but in stages. As an exercise I leave the reader to order the sequence as he or she considers appropriate!

Second, and following on immediately from this first rider, if there is an ordered acquisition of rights, it should display consistency. If children are assumed to display the competence required for one kind of right, they should not be refused another kind of right which presupposes the same, or even a lesser, degree of ability. It would not make sense, for instance, to deny a young person the right to refuse medical treatment but allow them to choose to die in the armed services of their state.

The liberationist may make one last move. He may concede that children do lack the capacities that are a prerequisite for the possession of rights. However, he can suggest that children should be permitted 'to *borrow* the capacities of others to secure whatever it is we are entitled to' (Cohen, H., 1980: 56). Child agents would advise their clients with a view to ensuring that the child's right is properly exercised. There are, however, various problems with this move. Most of these exactly parallel those besetting the idea of entrusting the choices of a child to a representative discussed earlier. First, who are to be the advisers? These may be selected by some fact, such as their biological kinship or their socially recognized role of guardianship, but this fact does not guarantee that they will be the best advisers. A parent is not, by the mere fact of parenthood, qualified to give her children the best advice. On the other hand, there is unlikely to be any clear fact of the matter as to who is the best adviser or what is the best advice. Indeed, the various adults who might best advise a child could well give conflicting advice. Second, how is one to determine what should guide the advice? Is it what the child herself would choose if competent to choose, or what is in the best interests of the child? The problems with understanding either determination will be further discussed later in this chapter. Third, is the child still free to act or not on the advice given? If the child is not so free, then the role of the adviser is a strictly paternalist one; the adviser is simply in a position to supplant the child's choice as to what is best for herself with her own choice as her adviser. If, on the other hand, the child *is* free to reject the adviser's advice, then the child is free to do what she wants anyway. This is so even though it has been conceded that she is not competent to recognize what is in her best interests. In this case, the role of adviser is superfluous.

One needs only to 'borrow' what one does not have. Not using what could be borrowed leaves one with the lack – and its consequences – that made the borrowing necessary. Conversely, if a child can distinguish good from bad advice, then the borrowing is unnecessary, since the child can give as good advice to herself as would be given to her by an adviser. However, in these circumstances, no adviser is needed, and this is precisely what Cohen denies.

Children's Rights and Adult Rights

If children can have at least some rights, what rights should they have? One important reason for asking, and for giving a satisfactory answer to, this question is a concern that the child's moral status should be adequately secured and protected. As we have seen, some, such as Onora O'Neill, believe that this is assured by discharging our obligations as adults to children. We have also seen above, in responding to the allegation of arbitrariness, that we can believe that there are things we ought not to do to children, just as there are things we ought not to do to animals, without believing that animals or children have rights. But children are not animals. They are human beings. Ought they not, then, to have the basic rights that human beings have?

One thought would be that, although children are entitled to the same moral consideration as adults, it does not follow that children should possess the same package of rights as adults. Since children are human beings they are surely entitled to the basic human rights. But there are some rights that adults possess which children cannot. This is a view defended by Brennan and Noggle (1997). The rights which adults possess are 'role-dependent rights'. These are rights associated with particular roles, and possession of the relevant right is dependent on an ability to play the role. Thus doctors have rights that their patients do not, and car-drivers have rights that those who have not passed their driving test do not. This argument is interesting not least because it does not provide, in respect of their rights, a fundamental distinction between adults and children. After all, some adults could conceivably possess no more than the basic rights possessed by children since they might have none of the abilities required to play any of the roles associated with the role-dependent rights.

However, it is not obvious that children *do* have the basic human rights that adults have. Central amongst these rights is that of self-determination – that is, the right to make choices in respect of one's own life. This right is the basis of derivative rights to marry, have sex, choose one's work, pursue a course of education and so on. But it is just this right that is normally denied to children, and it seems that Noggle and Brennan do deny, in effect, that children have this right. If parents can, as the authors think they may, overrule a child's life-choice, it is difficult to see how the right of choice nevertheless does not vanish (Brennan and Noggle, 1997: 16–17). If one adult were to deny that another adult could choose as she wished, it would be natural to describe this as a denial of the second adult's right of choice.

To say that children do not have all the basic human rights that adults do is not to deny them their status as humans. After all, it makes sense to insist that children, but not animals, have a basic right to life. Vegetarians who think it immoral to kill animals for food do not – as they could – protect animals from being killed by other animals. They do not enforce a duty of predatory species not to violate the rights of their animal victims. It also makes sense, as suggested, to say that children do not have an adult right of self-determination. It is controversial to say that children are 'persons', since, following John Locke (1961), this term denotes those possessed of moral agency and capable of being responsible for their actions. Weaker or stronger conceptions of 'personhood' would lead to the inclusion or exclusion of human beings at various ages from the category of 'person'. However, it is not controversial to state that children are human, and in saying this to insist that they are entitled to a certain moral regard.

Most who believe that adults have rights which children do not distinguish between liberty and welfare rights. Following Feinberg (1980), we can distinguish between rights that belong only to adults (A-rights), rights that are common to both adults and children (A-C rights), and rights that children alone possess

(C-rights). Thus a common position is that the A-rights include, centrally, the liberty rights, and that the A-C-rights include, centrally, the welfare rights. To repeat, liberty rights are rights of choice (how and whether to vote, what to say publicly, whether to practise a religion and which one, which if any association to join and so on) whereas welfare rights protect important interests (such as health, bodily integrity and privacy).

What might be included in the C-rights? Again, following Feinberg, we can distinguish two subclasses of C-rights. There are, first, those rights which children possess in virtue of their condition of childishness. Although Feinberg does not further divide this first subclass of C-rights, we can do so. First, there are the rights children have to receive those goods they are incapable of securing for themselves, and are incapable of so doing because of their childish dependence on adults. These goods might include food and shelter. Second, there are the rights to be protected against harms which befall children because of their childlike vulnerability and whose particular harmfulness is a function of a fact that they befall children. These harms might include abuse and neglect. Finally, there are goods that children should arguably receive just because they are children. The most central, and contentious, example is a child's right to be loved. This is not an A-C-right, but it is arguably a C-right and, indeed, is cited by many as such (MacCormick, 1976: 305). Various declarations of children's rights include such a right, and a respectable case can be made to meet the various objections normally raised against its attribution (Liao, 2000).

We might call these C-rights 'protection' rights since, in general, they seek to provide protection for children. Moreover, they do so because the state or condition of childhood calls forth, and requires, this protection. Nevertheless, we should take care to distinguish protection rights from welfare rights. Children, along with adults, have welfare rights, but the content of these will differ between children and adults simply because of the particular form that children's needs and circumstances take. For example, both children and adults have a welfare right to health care but, in the case of children but not that of adults, paediatric care and treatment is appropriate. However, that fact is no more significant than the fact that, amongst different adults, the proper form of health care should vary in line with their various disabilities, diseases and circumstances.

The Child's Right to Grow Up

The second subclass of C-rights are those which Feinberg characterizes as 'rights-in-trust' and which he thinks can be resumed under the single title of a 'right to an open future'. These are the rights given to the child in the person of the adult she will become. They are the rights whose protection ensures that, as an adult, she will be in a position to exercise her A- and A-C-rights to the maximal, or at least to a very significant, degree. They keep her future open. Such rights impose limits on the rights of parents and also impose duties on the part of the state to protect these rights.

A couple of things are worth noting about these rights-in-trust. First, Feinberg refers to these C-rights as 'anticipatory autonomy rights', which might suggest that they are only A-rights-in-trust. But he also speaks, within a page, of rights-in-trust of class C as protecting those future interests a child will have as an adult. This implies that they are also anticipatory *welfare* rights (Feinberg, 1980: 126–27). I shall thus assume, as stated above, that this subclass of C-rights ensures that the adult can later exercise both her A-rights (liberty) and her A-C-rights (welfare).

Second, we can raise the question of *how* open a child's future should be. Some interpret the demand for an education for an 'open future' as requiring individuals to acquire 'to the greatest possible extent' the capacity to choose between 'the widest possible variety of ways of life' (Arneson and Shapiro, 1996: 388). They correctly point out several objections to such a 'maximizing' interpretation. It may not be possible to quantify, in a determinate fashion, the number of options open to a future adult. Furthermore some fulfilling life choices are only available at the expense of denying the child a number of otherwise possible choices. For instance, a child intensively trained to realize his considerable innate musical abilities may be unable to pursue careers that would have been open to him in the absence of such a dedicated education. Let me add the following further criticisms. Requiring that a child be brought up to be able eventually to choose between as many options as possible may impose unreasonable burdens on parents. It also seems implausible to think that a child suffers if she is denied one, or even several, possible insignificant further options beyond some threshold number of choices. Is it really harmful to a child that she does not learn to play *all* of the orchestral instruments and is thereby denied the opportunity to pursue a solo career in those she does not?

Feinberg does sometimes talk only of the harms of closing off significant life choices. Yet he does also, on occasion, employ the language of maximization: '[Education] should send [the child] out into the adult world with as many open opportunities as possible, thus maximising his chances for self-fulfilment' (Feinberg, 1980: 135; see also 151). However, it seems much more plausible to suggest that a child should have *enough* autonomy to be able to make reasonable life choices. The preconditions of autonomy are both internal (a capacity to think for oneself, to acquire and appreciate relevant information, and a volitional ability to act independently) and external (the provision of a range of feasible and valuable options). In respect of both conditions it is perfectly possible to have a good sense of what counts as *adequate* autonomy, even if there is no clear bright line marking the point of sufficiency.

Closely related to Feinberg's idea of 'rights-in-trust' is Eekelaar's idea of a child's 'developmental' rights (Eekelaar, 1986b). These are the rights of a child to develop her potential so that she enters adulthood without disadvantage. Whereas Feinberg attributes the rights to the child's adult-self, the child holding them only in 'anticipatory' form, Eekelaar attributes the rights to the adult's child-self. Arguably, this makes no difference since the child and the adult are one and the same person. Although this is a metaphysically contentious claim (Parfit, 1984) let us grant that child and adult are merely distinct temporal stages of a single individual. Child and adult have thus the same interest in development.

However, child and adult do stand in an asymmetrical relationship to one another in a way that does not seem to be true of the different temporal stages of the same adult. After all, I can now exercise my liberty rights in such a fashion that at a later time I am not able to exercise these, and my welfare rights, to the same degree as I can now. I can, for instance, choose now to enter into a slavery contract or to engage in a dangerous sport that risks death or serious disability. A child, on the other hand, is denied the right to make choices that will fetter the adult exercise of her rights. This is justified by three thoughts. First, a child, unlike an adult, simply lacks the ability to make considered choices and should not have liberty rights. An adult can make unwise choices but is presumed to possess a general capacity, which the child lacks, to make wise choices. Or at least we think that an adult has a minimal capacity to make choices which the child lacks, even if a particular adult throughout her life makes suboptimal choices. Second, what is done or not done in childhood affects the *whole* of one's later life and does so in a way that is largely irreversible. Third, a life in which choices can be made is more valuable than one in which they cannot. So the preconditions for the possibility of such a life should be secured. That is just to say that the child must allow for the possibility of becoming its adult-self.

However, consider the case of a child who will not develop into an adult – say, someone who is suffering from a terminal disease that will prevent her living beyond the age of majority. Such a child lacks developmental rights. Or, rather, she has them but her circumstances do not allow for their protection. However, she does still have welfare and protection rights whose correlate duties can be discharged. Moreover, it is noteworthy that discharging these duties can serve what would, in the absence of the illness, have been her developmental interests.

When, for instance, we provide a child with health care or protect her from abuse we not only thereby serve her immediate interests as a child but we also ensure that she will grow into a mentally and physically healthy adult. At its simplest a child's welfare right not to be killed is a precondition of the very possibility of there being a future adult with any rights at all. Even the education of a child can be represented as not merely of instrumental worth to the future adult but of value to the child here and now. A child has an interest now in learning things and does so independently of what this might later mean for her future adult self (Coady, 1992: 51).

What kind of adult does her childhood self have an interest in developing into? The answer to this question is important not least for indicating appropriate constraints on any parental upbringing. I will not canvass all the possibilities here because we must acknowledge that the state has an interest in what kind of adult a child develops into, and a parent has an interest in seeing her children develop in certain ways.

Thus a full discussion of this question must wait until I have examined the perspectives of parent and state. However, I will note here a very influential and recognizably liberal view of what sort of adult a child has an interest in developing into – namely, an *autonomous* individual, one able independently to evaluate and to choose as appropriate her own ends. On the liberal view, a child is not autonomous but can, with the proper upbringing, become autonomous. This view is most directly contrasted with a conception of the individual as equipped with a set of values and beliefs, authoritatively acquired during its childhood as a result of its upbringing and not open to revision, or at least not open to any substantial revision. It is this contrast of views which I shall discuss further in the final chapter.

Returning to the case of the child with the terminal illness. She will not develop into an adult. If the child had a choice, could we say of her that she had a warranted interest in not developing into an adult? Grant that the child-Q and the adult-Q are two stages of one and the same individual. Could we speak of a conflict between the present interest of child-Q in staying a child and the future interest of adult-Q in child-Q developing into her later adult self? The latter interest seems perfectly straightforward. However, it is at least controversial whether all adults *do* have an interest in growing up. We simply assume that, for human beings, existence is preferable to non-existence. However, Benatar (1997), has argued that it is true of human beings that it is better that they never existed than that they do exist. It would then be true that children would not regret coming into existence and that existing adults are duty-bound not to procreate. Although such a proposition will certainly strike most people as wildly implausible, it may nevertheless be true of *some* human beings that not growing into adulthood and ceasing to exist is better than becoming an adult. This might be the case, for instance, of somebody facing the prospect of a life of unrelieved, extreme pain and misery. Nevertheless, let us grant that, in general, adults do have an interest in their child-selves developing into adults. What sense, then, can we make of the *child*'s interest in staying a child?

A marvellous fictional illustration of the issue is provided by the famous J.M. Barrie play, *Peter Pan*, whose subtitle, significantly, is 'The Boy Who Would Not Grow Up' (Barrie, 1995). *Peter Pan* is frequently invoked, and all too often wrongly remembered, as being a charming fairy tale of the wonders of childhood. In fact, the work is simultaneously a play for children and a play for adults. In its latter guise it offers a subtle social satire of gender roles as well as reflections on time, eternity and the relationship between fantasy and reality. As a play about childhood, if not for children, it does not offer a naïve celebration of eternal youth – far from it.

The play's eponymous hero inhabits an impossible world, literally 'NeverLand', where no child grows up but can play games forever. However, it is also a timeless world without memory and with an ignorance of both death (no more than an 'awfully big adventure') and sex. Thus Peter does not recognize the burgeoning erotic interest displayed in him by Wendy. He can only see all 'ladies' as mothers. It is a very Freudian implication of the play that it is the knowledge of sex and death that transforms life into 'an awfully big adventure'.

The character of Wendy Darling provides the most direct contrast with Peter Pan. At one point in the play, Peter Pan (the child who plays at being an adult) and Wendy (the child who will eventually be an adult) pretend to parent the Lost Boys of NeverLand. The former does so in ignorance of the experience, and blind to its significance. The latter, by contrast, does so in anticipation of the experience and aware of its value. Peter Pan chose 'not to grow up' because he heard his parents 'talking of what I was to be when I became a man' (1.1: 397–8) and he refuses the adoption proffered by Wendy's mother because he does not 'want to go to school and learn solemn things'. He immediately thereafter repeats for the second time in the play his simpleminded insistence that 'I just want to be a little boy and to have fun' (1.1: 398–99; 4.1: 236–37; 5.2: 134–35).

The 'riddle' of Peter Pan's being is that he cannot 'get the hang of the thing'. His wilful refusal to enter the world of time, maturity, knowledge and adult responsibilities is tragic but also futile. For Barrie, the escape from time, and death, is an evasion of knowledge, reality, and the affirmation of life. It is no response to our human condition. In Barrie's 'afterthought', the mini-play 'When Wendy Grew Up', the contrast drawn between a mature, married Wendy with children of her own and a permanently childish Peter who cannot even recall his own earlier adventures is clearly intended to display the impoverished condition of the latter. As an editor of Barrie's play, Peter Hollindale, notes,'Wendy is a citizen of reality rather than illusion and exists in time, contrasting with the frozen eternity of Peter's youthfulness' (Barrie 1995: xiii). It is the citizens of reality, not the eternally youthful, who win the day.

It should also be remembered that, in Barrie's fiction, Peter Pan dwells apart from our world in an impossible land of eternal childhood where his companions are other children who also will never grow up. But our world is the real one. Within this world the child does not, like Peter Pan, have an interest in always being a child. It is one thing to be a child forever in a child's world; it is quite another to remain a child in our adult world. Childhood is something best appreciated by the child. It is also something that needs to be left behind. In the words of Paul, 'When I was a child, I spoke as a child, I understood as a child, I thought as a child: but when I became a man I put away these childish things' (1 Corinthians 13:11).

Best Interests

If children are not thought to have the A-rights, and, chiefly, do not have the liberty rights to choose for themselves how to conduct their lives, nevertheless they are not morally abandoned to their own devices. In the first place, it is a standard principle of child welfare law and policy that the 'best interests' of a child should be promoted and it forms a key article of the United Nations Convention on the Rights of the Child. Article 3.1 states that '[i]n all actions concerning children, whether undertaken by public or private social welfare institutions, courts of law, administrative authorities or legislative bodies, the best interests of the child shall be a primary consideration' (United Nations, 1989). The principle has also been a cornerstone of British legislation affecting children, although we should note that, in the Children Act, the relevant principle is that 'the child's welfare shall be the court's paramount consideration' (Children Act 1989 I, 1(1)).

Second, it is also a key principle of British law that children's views on matters affecting their interests shall be heard and that these views shall be accorded a weight that is proportionate to the child's maturity and understanding of the relevant issues. This is enshrined in the Gillick principle which governs the competence of children and young persons to consent to medical treatment. The relevant article of the United Nations Convention, Article 12.1 asserts that: 'States Parties shall assure to the child who is capable of forming his or her own views the right to express those views freely in all matters affecting the child, the views of the child being given due weight in accordance with the age and maturity of the child' (United Nations, 1989).

I will say something in turn about each of these principles. First let me discuss the best interest principle, henceforward the BIP. As noted above, the principle has been given different explicit formulations. Indeed, we should note that the principle's possible definitions vary in at least two important dimensions: what is being given weight, and how much weight it is being given. Thus we may speak of a child's '*best* interests' or simply of a child's 'interests' or 'welfare'. The former is the more familiar version of the principle and it is this understanding of the principle that will be discussed. The difficulties with this maximizing interpretation will be considered in due course.

As to the weight of the principle, the distinct terms 'paramount' and 'primary' have been employed, along with either the definite or indefinite article, to qualify the consideration that should be given to a child's (best) interests. There are therefore at least four possible weightings: (a) the paramount; (b) a paramount; (c) the primary; (d) a primary. A fifth – that a child's (best) interests should merely be 'a consideration' – is otiose. *Some* consideration should obviously be given to a child's interests; the question, however, is how much. I shall understand the distinction between 'paramount' and 'primary' as follows. A consideration that is paramount outranks *and* trumps all other considerations. It is, in effect, the only consideration determinative of an outcome. A consideration that is 'primary' is a leading consideration, one that is first in rank among several. But although no considerations outrank a primary consideration there may be other considerations of equal, first rank. Furthermore a leading consideration does not trump even if it outranks all other considerations. A primary consideration is not the only consideration determinative of an outcome.

So it should be evident that (a) and (b) are equivalent, and that the real contrast is between a paramount consideration that trumps all others and a primary one that need not. In effect, the interesting choice is between (a) and (d) – that is, one between a child's (best) interests being the only consideration and their being an important, but not the sole, consideration. Indeed a debate took place as to which of these two versions should be included within the UN Convention on the Rights of the Child with the weaker formulation being eventually adopted (Alston, 1994: 12). The difficulties with the idea that a child's (best) interests are the only consideration in the determination of any issues will be discussed further in due course.

I should also note, before proceeding further, that we can speak either of 'a' child or, more generally, of 'children'. There is a difference between considering how in some matter the child most directly concerned is affected and considering how any policy or action in respect of that one child may also have consequences for other children. Indeed, we might consider how any policy or action at all has implications – even if very indirect and attentuated – for all children. However, it is plausible to construe a use of 'children' within a formulation of the BIP as requiring us to attend to the impact of a policy, practice or activity upon those young persons most obviously and directly affected. The BIP's origins are to be found in custody disputes where the law had to make a determination in respect of a couple's children. Even if there were several children, the court had to decide in respect of each individual child what was the most appropriate course of action. The provenance of the BIP shows itself in the continued use of the singular term 'child'.

There is a still further question of how we should understand the scope of the best interests principle. The BIP has operated in at least two important domains (Kopelman, 1997a). One is in the medical context when determining which option should be selected for an ill or diseased child. The second is in custody disputes following the separation or divorce of the child's guardians. Here, where there is unresolved argument as to who should now raise the child, the court must decide. However, beyond these two specified domains, the BIP has also been given broader application in respect of all policies and laws affecting children. This is certainly what the UN Convention Article 3.1 appears to require.

There are at least two kinds of difficulty in accepting the BIP (for a summary of various criticisms see Kopelman, 1997b). The first of these concerns the import of the principle, and the second concerns how we should interpret 'best interests'. Let me take each in turn. As to its import, the BIP is, in the first instance, a maximizing maxim. It requires that the *best* shall be done for a child and not simply that good or enough must be done. One must act 'so as to promote maximally the good' of the child (Buchanan and Brock, 1989: 10).

In some contexts, where the BIP operates there appears to be a determinate number of options, and perhaps even only a pair of options. This seems to be the case in custody disputes and medical decision-making. Where each divorced parent lays claim to exclusive custody to the child, no other party has any claim and no compromise is possible, there are only two possibilities. In this context, the better option is the best. The same is true when the decision is simply whether or not to pursue or to abstain from a course of medical treatment. By contrast, in the area of general policy affecting children there seem to be very many different possibilities. Yet even with custody and medical decisions we can expand the range of possible options. Thus what might be *best* for the child is not that she is cared for by either of the parents claiming custody, but that she is adopted by someone else entirely. Again, what might be *best* for the child is not that she receive the medical treatment on offer rather than not do so, although it may well be *better* that she does. What is best is that she is treated by the most skilled medical personnel within the finest medical facility, with no expense spared, and so on.

But, then, the obvious criticism of the BIP is that it is

unfeasibly demanding of agencies charged with the care of children. Should we really demand that our law and policy-makers do the best for children rather than charge them with doing enough for children? We do not, it seems, require parents to promote their children's best interests. Nor should we. Indeed, the standard principles of child welfare policy, even when they include a version of the best interests maxim, do not stipulate that a child's parents shall do more than ensure that the child receives a threshold of care. Beyond that, parents are not normally required maximally to promote their child's interests, and indeed they have considerable discretion as to how they raise the child. So the BIP is not best interpreted as a maximizing principle. We should do so much for a child; we should not be obliged to do everything that, in principle, we might do.

A second problem of the import of the BIP is that it does not, as it stands, take account of the interests of others. First, I might be able to improve the situation of child A but only at the cost of worsening that of child B. It is natural to think that the interests of all children should be weighed equally. Hence the BIP ought to be read as requiring us impartially to promote the best interests of each and every child. Of course the BIP directs courts, social workers or medical practitioners in some case to promote the interests of a particular child. But this should not be done by treating the interests of any other child who might be affected as having no value or a lesser value than those of the particular child attended to. It would not be reasonable to expect that parents should view the interests of their own children as having the same weight as that of other children. It *is* reasonable to ask policy-makers and care professionals to do so.

Second, we cannot be required to promote the best interests of a child over and above, and without regard to, the interests of any relevant adult. It might be in the best interests of a child that her guardian give up every waking minute to her care, but no adult should have to sacrifice her own welfare for that of her child. The BIP should thus be interpreted so as to give at least equal consideration to the interests or to the well-being of any adults affected by policies and actions promoting the child's welfare.

The second set of difficulties surrounding the BIP concern the interpretation of 'best interests'. One way of understanding this phrase is by reference to what a child would choose for herself under specified hypothetical circumstances. We could call this the 'hypothetical choice' interpretation of the BIP. The other way of understanding 'best interests' is simply through offering an account of what is, as a matter of fact, best for the child – an account which is distinct from, and independent of, the child's desires, whether actual or hypothetical. Let us call this the 'objectivist' interpretation of the BIP. I will examine each interpretation in turn.

The 'objectivist' interpretation of the BIP is beset by a number of difficulties. Some urge that what is best for any child is necessarily indeterminate. There certainly is no fact of the matter in this regard for we must attach values to the options and their outcomes in respect of any choice of action towards a child. However, it will be said that, independently of questions of value, we cannot, with certainty, determine what is best for a child. We cannot, in practice, make complete and accurate assessments of what will be the outcome of each and every policy option that we might adopt in respect of a child (Mnookin, 1979). How can we know with certainty whether this child will flourish if raised by this set of parents rather than by some others in an alternative setting? Even where we are seeking to rank the outcomes of the options within a simple custody dispute between a mother and father, things may prove impossibly difficult. After all, any number of things may happen if the child is in the mother's custody, and the same is true if the child is given to the father. The BIP is indeterminate even where there are only two possible decisions to be made (Elster, 1989: 134–39).

This difficulty can be spelled out in the following fashion. Imagine that indeterminacy afflicts each of the four conditions of a full decision procedure (Parker, 1994: 29–31). For a decision to be made, the possible options must be known, the possible outcomes of each possible option must be known, the probabilities of each possible outcome occurring must be known, and the value of each outcome must be known. Independently of the uncertainty in respect of the last condition – the value of the outcomes – it is probably true that there is uncertainty in respect of the other three conditions. However, it is not clear why the problem is one that is especially, or uniquely, true of policies affecting children. *Any* political or legal determination is going to face such indeterminacy in the specification of choices and their outcomes.

Of course, once we put values back into the equation there is, arguably, clear indeterminacy. Moral pluralists will hold that it is not possible to rank as better or worse different kinds of life. They will say that it is not possible, in principle, to compare the lives of the fearless adventurer, contemplative scholar and creative artist. Each realizes its own distinctive, but strictly incommensurable, set of human excellences. How, then, can we say that there is a best life for a child to grow into, rather than a range of equally possible yet incomparable lives?

The pluralist claim is not directed uniquely at children. The value of some at least of the lives of adults are, for the pluralist, strictly incomparable. I will then, for the sake of argument, deny the pluralist claim and assume that there is for each and every child a uniquely best life that she could be brought to lead. There is a still further difficulty. Even if moral pluralism as a claim about what is of ultimate objective value is set aside, the fact remains that we do happen to disagree in our basic values. Indeed, it is a commonplace of contemporary moral and political philosophy that equally sincere, conscientious and reasonable individuals espouse fundamentally different, and frequently conflicting, views about morality. As a society we may be able to agree about what is a poor, neglectful or abusive upbringing, but we are likely to be in irresolvable disagreement about what is 'good', and even what is 'better', parenting (McGough, 1995: 375). We just cannot agree what is in a child's best interests.

The fact of extensive disagreement about what is best for children, or for a child, is often set in the context of broader cultural disagreements about morality in general. It is said that the BIP is subverted, or at least rendered deeply problematic, by the existence of these deep and pervasive cultural disagreements (An-Na'im, 1994; Alston (ed.) 1994). One must be careful here. The statement 'what is best for a child is different in different cultures' is, in fact, ambiguous; it can mean at least two different things. In the first place, the phrase 'in different cultures' may be interpreted as meaning something like 'in different circumstances'. Most moral philosophers will acknowledge that a universal moral principle that all are agreed upon can nevertheless have differential application in differently specified circumstances. Here we do not dispute what, in general terms, is best for a child. But we do recognize that what it is best to do for any individual child will depend on the particular conditions in which that child finds herself. For example, imagine that we all assent to the principle that 'every child should receive the best possible education its society can provide'. That is consistent with its being the case that the best each society can provide for its young varies. It is also consistent with its being the case that the best education in one society will have a substantively different form and content from that in another. If an education prepares a child for adulthood in its own culture, then it may not be appropriate in non-literate societies for a child to learn to read and write. Or at least it may not be best for literacy to have primacy in the education of children within these societies.

On the other hand, what is meant by the statement 'what is best for a child is different in different cultures' may be that there is no general agreement across cultures about what is best for a child. Each culture has its own understanding of what is in a child's best interests. This is not a question of applying the same, agreed version of a single BIP to different cultural contexts. Rather there is a BIP specific to each culture. One culture, for instance, thinks that it is in every child's best interests to receive the best possible education it can. Another believes that whilst this is true of boys, it is best for girls that they prepare for a life of domestic service that does not need any formal education. If this claim is taken to be one about the impossibility in principle of a single BIP then it amounts to an assertion of moral relativism. What culture A thinks is best for any child *is* best for any child. What culture B thinks is best for any child – even though it contradicts what culture A thinks best – is also what *is* best for any child. Moral relativism, in some form, has its defenders but its attendant problems are well documented (Wong, 1998).

If the claim 'what is best for a child is different in different cultures' is a report of cultural difference – what each culture *believes* to be best for its children – then it is still consistent with the BIP having a single universal content. What is best for children is the same whatever the culture, and allowing for the variation in application of the same principle to different contexts. It is just that some cultures do not adhere to the BIP in this form. However, matters are clearly not that simple. It is one thing to acknowledge in principle that there must be a single BIP; it is quite another to find agreement on what that principle is. The discussions surrounding the formulation of international conventions of human rights have been notoriously beset by significant, and culturally-based, differences of moral and political outlook. The United Nations Convention on the Rights of the Child was no different (LeBlanc, 1995).

There is always also a danger that the global adoption of one understanding of the BIP – or indeed, generally, a view as to what rights are possessed by children – will be regarded by some as an act of cultural imperialism, whereby a dominant culture imposes its moral understandings upon subordinate cultures. Finally, it need not be clear which version of the claim that 'what is best for a child is different in different cultures' is appropriate. Consider a culture that attaches a special significance to the child's inheritance of a particular identity and to her participation in certain practices that honour or signify that identity. If it is argued from within the culture that the child should participate in these practices is this a case of a quite specific understanding of what is in the child's best interests or merely a local application of a single, agreed BIP to the individual circumstances of this culture? Does this culture have a particularistic moral understanding of what is best for all children? Or does it share with other cultures a view of what is best for children, which it then applies to its own local context?

Even within single cultures which share a broad understanding of what is in a child's best interests there will still be some measure of disagreement. For instance, within Western societies there are continuing disputes about whether it is morally proper to smack a child. Given all of this, who is to decide? We should beware of thinking that a parent knows best. Qualification to judge what is best for a child requires both knowledge of the child in question *and* an ability to form generally reliable evaluative judgements about the good life. Even if we grant that this last ability can be measured and that good judges can be identified, this will not show that the parent should choose for the child. Of course, parents may claim that they are entitled to choose for their children because, and simply because, they are their parents. That is, they assert that they have parental rights over their children. This claim will be considered further in the next chapter. What parents cannot claim is to be better judges of their children's best interests than any other potential adult guardians because, and simply because, they are the children's parents.

Parents may be able successfully to argue that they know their children better than anyone else, by reason of sharing genes and hence character traits, or in consequence of an unparalleled commitment to care for, and hence to try to understand, their own offspring. Moreover, a parent's unconditional love for her child disposes her to bring it about that her child will have the good life, even if that entails significant sacrifices on the part of the parent. But that still leaves it unsettled how well a parent can identify the good life. Parents are not qualified, simply in virtue of being parents, to know what is needed for any child to lead the good life. Parents do not, as such, know what is best.

It might, however, be argued that it is in the best interests of the child that the child's parents choose what is in the child's best interests. This is not because what the parent chooses is actually best – either as a rule or always – but because it is best that the parent chooses. That is, we may think that it is always best that a child receive a stable upbringing by guardians unconditionally committed to the love and care of their children. What is involved in the provision of such an upbringing is just the making of choices for the child by the parents, subject, of course, to familiar constraints. This general claim may be true, but it provides, at most, a presumption in favour of *some* adult or adults who can provide stable and enduring care for a child being entrusted with the making of the child's choices.

In other words, the general claim shows only that children ought to have parents or guardians. It does not settle the question of who these guardians should be. A child must be brought up by *somebody* who cares for and loves her. It is conceivable that any number of people could fulfil this role. There is a further question of who is best fitted to be the child's actual parents. This is not answered simply by appealing to the value of the child having some parents rather than none. It might be the child's natural parents, but it need not be.

Given the difficulties afflicting the 'objectivist' interpretation of the BIP, can we still make any use of it? We could, of course, construe it in minimalist fashion. So we might simply say the following. In any context of decision-making about a child there are a number of salient, practicable options. Amongst these one should choose that which is evidently best. Rather than seeking beyond these options for what may, in principle, be the best for this child, we should strive to do what we can now that at least improves her situation from the status quo ante. This is some way from the strict maximalist construal of the BIP, but it has the considerable advantages of realism and practicability.

Before going on to look at the 'hypothetical choice' interpretation of the BIP, we should note the following about the operation of the principle. First, in practice, the BIP is applied where there is a pressing reason to ask 'What should we do for this child?'. For most of the time and in respect of most children, we can trust to the benevolent dispositions of parents and presume that our existing practices, laws and policies do, on the whole, work for the general benefit of children. We do not, that is, take literally the injunction to ask of *every* child and on *any* matter affecting her, what is for the best.

Second, the practical import of the operation of the BIP has been twofold. First, it has required that people attend to the issues of what is good for a child and, in particular, what is good for this uniquely individual child. It has thus acted as a corrective to a previously longstanding failure even to think about the needs and well-being of children. Second, it has given expression to a decisive shift away from the assumption that children are simply the property of their parents or that, in respect of a child, it is only her parents' wishes that count. It has forced adults to take into account what matters to and for the child itself.

By contrast with an 'objectivist' interpretation of the BIP, we can understand what is best for a child in terms of a child's hypothetical choices. Strictly speaking, a hypothetical-choice interpretation of the BIP amounts to a distinct principle. It is one Buchanan and Brock define as that of the 'substituted judgement' – 'acting according to what the incompetent individual, if competent, would choose' (Buchanan and Brock, 1989: 10). However, it is natural to think that what is best for someone is what they themselves would choose if fully informed and deliberating fully rationally. Thus a striking and influential thought in this context is that we choose what is best for the child if we choose for the child as the child would choose for herself if the child were adult. For instance, John Rawls thinks the following formulation defines the acceptable paternalism of a guardian's treatment of his child: 'We must choose for others as we have reason to believe they would choose for themselves if they were at the age of reason and deciding rationally' (Rawls, 1972: 209). This apparently simple formulation is in fact susceptible of three quite different interpretations, each of which brings with it its own problems. In each case, we are seeking to specify the adult person who chooses for the child.

We might first mean that we should choose for this child as the particular adult the child will become would choose. However, this does not determine a unique choice for, crucially, the nature of the particular adult that the child will become depends on the choices that are made for her whilst a child. We can conceive of each of the different adult-selves the child might develop into approving, respectively, of the different choices made for its child-self – choices which were responsible for the development of these different selves. Let us take a very basic example. Should we allow the child to go off and play football with his peers, or require him to attend his violin lessons? The child who is allowed to play football becomes a well-paid sportsman who, retrospectively, approves of the decision to free him from music lessons which hampered his ability to develop his footballing skills. On the other hand, the child who is made to practise his violin progresses to a fulfilling solo career. *This* adult – by contrast with the footballer he did not become – approves of the enforced musical education away from football that allowed him to have such a career.

In each case, we assume that the choice made for the child makes a significant difference to the kind of adult the child grows into. If this seems unduly fanciful, assume that what is at stake is a patterned set of choices – indeed such a set as would reflect the parenting style and outlook specific to particular guardians. What would the child, if at his age of reason, choose? It is once again simply unclear. Here there is a general point about paternalistic interventions that may be described as 'self-justifying'. Self-justifying paternalism is paternalistic behaviour which effects its own justification in that it brings about the very change of self whose retrospective consent to the interventions validates them (Archard, 1993b).

The second sense we might give to the phrase 'choose for the child as the child would if adult' is by thinking of the situation in which the choice confronts the child, and then choosing as an adult would. The person who chooses for the child is *any* adult. This will serve well enough for some choices where there is no doubt as to what a rational adult would choose. In classic adult–child paternalistic scenarios we are not unclear or undecided about what we as adults should do. Would a rational adult choose to stick her hand in the fire, walk out into the traffic, or eat whatever was placed in front of her? However, if the adult is confronted with other sorts of choice, the answer is far less clear. Faced with our imagined choice between playing football and a music lesson how would the adult choose? Here, different adults will presumably choose differently in the same situation. The adult who prefers football to music will choose the former; the adult who prefers music will choose otherwise.

This leads us, then, to the third possible interpretation. The adult person who chooses for the child is an adult analogue of the child. This is not the child's future adult-self, which as we have seen is indeterminate, but this child made into an adult version of itself. That is, we do not imagine this child developing in the future into its particular adult-self. Rather, we imagine a mature or grown-up version of this child now making choices. This interpretation, however, will still not work. Adopting a simple and familiar belief–desire model we might, as a first approximation, think that this adult version of the child still has the child's beliefs and desires but now possesses adult powers of ratiocination. This adult version is able rationally to choose so as most efficiently to realize the child's preferences. But this will not lead the adult version of the child to choose rationally. The child who wants to visit Santa Claus whom she believes lives in Lapland will choose to go to Lapland if she chooses as her adult analogue would choose for her.

We might modify the model further by envisaging a further process of instantaneous maturation. Thus an adult version of the child not only now has adult powers of ratiocination but also has lost her childish beliefs and childish desires; it has had such beliefs and desires filtered out. However, first, it is not clear what remains of the child in any choice situation rendered hypothetical in this fashion, for the child just is someone who has these childish beliefs and desires. What is it to be a child if not to think and want as a child does? Second, it is entirely indeterminate what should replace these beliefs and desires. If the adult version of the child does not want to visit Santa Claus and does not believe that he exists, what *does* she want and think? We are left with the indeterminacy of the formulation, 'any adult', which the second possible account of 'choose as an adult' offered.

These varying interpretations of what it is to choose for a child as an adult, and their attendant difficulties, display the insuperable problem of construing the best interests of a child in terms of the hypothetically adult choices the child would make. In the final analysis, the problems are due to the following basic fact. In the cases of adults paternalistically choosing for other adults, and where the paternalism is warranted by a temporary failure of reason, we can have a determinate sense of how the adult would have chosen in the absence of the failure. If she had known that the bridge was unsafe, she would have chosen not to cross it. If she was not persuaded by the influence of the drug to think she could fly, she would not have decided to jump off the tall building. And so on.

However, in the case of children we cannot cash out these hypothetical conditionals. We do not know what a child would choose if possessed of adult rational powers of choice because what makes a child a child is just her lack of such powers (her ignorance, inconstant wants, inconsistent beliefs and limited powers of ratiocination). At the same time, we cannot ask how an adult would choose if in the child's situation just because an adult would not be in that situation, or would not be in a *child's* situation. We must, in short, choose for a child because a child cannot choose for herself, and we must choose what is best for a child not what some imagined adult version of the child would choose for herself. Nevertheless we must recognize, as has already been pointed out, that there is no determinate fact of the matter as to what is in a child's best interests.

The Right to be Heard

The right to be heard is a valuable right. What makes it valuable is that there is a point to making one's views known and, further, that making one's views known makes a difference. It matters to me that I can speak out on political questions. It matters also, and probably more, if what I say leads to the changes I favour. Correlatively, I do not want to be silenced nor do I want the statement of my views to be ineffectual. As a further general point, it is clear that there will always be some issues on which it is more important that I be allowed to speak and that what I say about these issues carries weight in determining outcomes. Those are the issues that matter to me, and the more they matter the more important it is that I have the freedom to speak about them and be heard.

How is it with the child's right to be heard? It will be important for the child to be listened to. But it is also important that the child is *heard* in the sense that her views are given due consideration and may influence what is done. Note that the child's right to be heard on matters affecting her own interests is a substitute for the liberty right to make one's own choices. The right to be heard is only a right to have the opportunity to influence the person who will otherwise choose for the child. The power to make those choices resides with the adult guardian or representative of the child. All the child retains is the right to try to motivate that adult to choose as the child herself would choose if she was allowed to.

Article 12.1 of the United Nations Convention on the Rights of the Child not only accords the child the right freely to express its views on matters affecting the child. It also, and crucially, gives the child an assurance that these views will be given 'due weight in accordance with the age and maturity of the child'. What might that mean? We can begin to answer this question by considering the celebrated English legal judgment in the

Gillick case (1986). This judgment has been extensively, if not exhaustively, discussed and has also been highly influential in matters relating to the consent of children to medical treatment. I shall not be concerned with how best legally to interpret the judgment nor with the various legalistic disputes that have surrounded it. Rather, I shall use the judgment as an illuminating introduction into the difficulties of understanding what it is to give due weight to a child's own views.

The *Gillick* judgment arose from the dissatisfaction of a mother with the failure of her local health authority to withdraw an advisory circular to the area's doctors. This advised doctors that they could counsel and inform young girls under the age of 16 about sexual matters, as well as provide them with contraception and that they could do this without the consent of the child's parents. The mother, Victoria Gillick, went to court to have the circular declared unlawful. The final judgment by the House of Lords was that the circular was not unlawful. A key issue, relevant to the present discussion, concerned the proper relationship between the child's right to decide for herself and the parent's right to decide for the child.

In deciding in favour of the health authority one of the Law Lords, Lord Scarman, made a statement crucial to his finding and one that has subsequently been much cited. It is worth reproducing:

> The underlying principle of the law ... is that parental right yields to the child's right to make his own decisions when he reaches a sufficient understanding and intelligence to be capable of making up his own mind on the matter requiring decision.
>
> I would hold that as a matter of law the parental right to determine whether or not their minor child below the age of 16 will have medical treatment terminates if and when the child achieves a sufficient understanding and intelligence to enable him to understand fully what is proposed. (*Gillick*, [1986] AC 112, 186, 188–89.)

What Lord Scarman meant has been disputed both in subsequent legal judgments and by commentators. Some of these disputed meanings will be rehearsed, others are not strictly relevant to the present discussion. There are two questions to be answered. First, how should we think of the significance of the child's achievement in this context? Second, what is meant by 'sufficient understanding and intelligence'?

First, then, what does it mean for a child to reach a particular point in their development? There are two ways in which we could interpret the idea of a child's displaying a certain level of understanding and intelligence. We could term these the threshold and proportionality readings. In turn, there are two possible versions of the threshold, a strong and a weak one. On the strong threshold interpretation a child under the age of majority nevertheless can secure the liberty right of someone at or over that age if she displays sufficient understanding and intelligence. This needs careful qualification. The child acquires such a right in respect of 'the matter requiring decision'. The child does not acquire a right to decide on *all* matters affecting her interests, only on those concerning which she displays sufficient understanding and intelligence. This qualification is assumed in what follows.

According to this account, then, there are two thresholds for the acquisition of an adult liberty right. One is the passing of the age of majority; the other is the exhibition of sufficient cognitive ability before that age is reached. These are two different kinds of threshold. One becomes either a 'mature minor' or a major. In so far as they are consistent with one another, it must be that age functions in the majority threshold as a reliable indicator of a certain level of cognitive ability. It is notable, thus, that an 18-year-old, if 18 is the age of majority, is presumed, without being tested, to have the ability that a younger person is required to manifest. However, whichever threshold is crossed, the young person who crosses it possesses the liberty right of an adult. When Lord Scarman says that 'parental right yields to the child's right' he means, on this interpretation, that the young person's liberty right to decide for herself succeeds and completely replaces the prior right of the parent to decide for her. This parental right of choice 'terminates' – that is, ceases to exist – once the threshold has been passed.

On the weak threshold interpretation a mature minor, unlike an immature minor, has a power to determine what shall happen to her. But it is a power that does not amount to the full liberty right possessed by an adult or by a mature minor on the strong threshold interpretation. That the mature minor has a view as to what shall happen to her does not settle the matter as to what ought to happen to her. There is also the question of what the parent would choose and of what is in the best interests of the child. Some interpreted Lord Scarman to intend that the parent retains a right of choice which is not replaced. Instead, this right 'yields' to the child's right only in the sense that it is now outweighed by the child's right.

This seems unclear and unpersuasive. If a child has a right to do Ø then others are under a duty to assist the child or at least not to obstruct her in the performance of Ø should the child decide to do Ø. 'Others' includes the child's parents. But if the parents *do* have a right to determine what their child shall do then they cannot, at the same time, be under any kind of duty in respect of the child's actions. Having such a right means that if they decide that the child shall not do Ø, then everyone else is duty-bound not to prevent its being the case that the child not do Ø. It seems, then, that if the child does have a right of choice over its actions, then the parents' 'right' of choice terminates and does not just 'yield' in the sense of being outweighed.

Indeed, it is probably inaccurate in this context even to talk of rights, either of the parent or of the child. Some deny that rights can conflict. Those who admit the possibility restrict it to cases in which one individual's right to X conflicts with another individual's right to Y. That is, they imagine such cases as one in which my right to walk a country path in peace and quiet conflicts with your right to ride a noisy motorbike down that same path. They do not allow for cases in which two distinct individuals both have rights with the same content – that is, rights to the very same thing. In this present case what is within the scope of any putative right is what the child shall be allowed to do. Both the child and the parent are supposed to have rights in respect of this same content. This makes very little sense. It makes far more sense to say that, if the child does have the right, then the parent does not. However, on the weak threshold interpretation, a child who crosses the threshold may only have a power – at most, a quasi-right if you will – of choice. This has a certain weight, but the wishes of the parents in respect of the child's actions also have a certain weight.

Talk of such weightings implies the following. The child's views as to what shall happen to her have a certain presumptive weight once the threshold, on the weak interpretation, has been passed. Before this threshold was passed the child's views carried no official weight. Nevertheless the child's views do not now settle the matter of what shall happen. Other considerations must be weighed in the balance. Imagine, then, that a court must, in any particular case, weigh the child's views, the parents' views and the state's views of what is in the best interests of the child. For ease of expression I will entitle these, respectively, CV, PV, and BI.

The manner in which this weighing can be done is complex. All three elements in the balance could be regarded as being of equal weight. Thus if PV coincides with CV this is sufficient to outweigh a contrary BI. Or if CV coincides with BI then this is sufficient to outweigh a contrary PV. Similarly, a coincident CV and BI would outweigh PV. However, if none of the three parties agrees, then no determinate outcome is indicated. One could – to adopt a different perspective – consider that the three elements are *not* of equal weight. A plausible ranking order would be one in which CV has a greater weight than either BI or PV. If CV weighs less than PV, then parental choices have in no way 'yielded' to a child's wishes. Further if CV weighs less than BI, it is not clear that the state is giving any weight to a child's wishes. For, in such a case, all that in effect matters is what the state thinks best for the child *whatever* the child herself thinks. (There is, as the discussion of *parens patriae* in Chapter 3 reveals, reason to think this is nevertheless how British law understands the role of BI.) This suggested ranking leaves open the possibility that BI and PV are sufficiently weighty, if conjoined, to outweigh CV. It also leaves open the weight of BI in relation to PV.

It should by now be more than evident that the weak threshold interpretation is beset by ambiguities and by a general lack of clarity. On the proportionality interpretation, by contrast, the child's power to determine what shall happen to her is proportionate to her level of understanding and intelligence. The more understanding and intelligence she displays, the more her views as to what shall happen to her weigh in the balance of considerations determining what shall indeed happen to her. These considerations comprise once again PV, CV and BI – and we should perhaps add the third-party concerns of those other than the child and parent. On the proportionality interpretation CV weighs the stronger, the more understanding and intelligence the child displays.

The key difference between the threshold and the proportionality interpretations is as follows. On the threshold interpretation, once a child has achieved a certain level of competence her views as to what shall happen to her have a determinate weight, either amounting to a liberty right of choice (on the strong version) or (on the weak version) being counted in the balance against her parents' views and the state's judgement of her best interests. On the proportionality interpretation, the child's views progressively increase in weight as she gains a greater competence to choose for herself. They increase up to the acquisition of a full liberty right of choice. Of course, it need not be inconsistent to think of a child's abilities in both proportionate and threshold terms. One might thus believe that, up to a certain point, a child's increasing cognitive abilities give her views ever greater weight in the overall balance of factors determining what shall be done to her. However, once a certain level of ability has been reached, the child acquires a quasi-right or a right proper to choose for herself

In the *Gillick* judgment the use of the language of sufficiency strongly suggests a threshold interpretation, although it could obviously be in either the weak or strong form. It is standard now to speak of a young person who does manifest enough understanding and intelligence as 'Gillick competent'. A child who is declared 'Gillick competent' has thus reached a level of cognitive ability that either entitles her to an unqualified right of choice or to a certain degree of respect for her choices that must be weighed in the balance against considerations of parental choice and her best interests.

On either the threshold or the proportionality account we need a measure of that ability that marks the threshold or is simply progressively acquired. How much intelligence and understanding, for instance, is sufficient? We can acknowledge a degree of decision relativity in any cognitive capacity. The intelligence required to tot up a shopping bill is less than that needed to understand nuclear physics. Similarly, it takes more to understand what is involved in deciding to have sex with someone than it does to understand what is involved in deciding what to cook for dinner. We can recognize this without believing that any such ability is intermittent –

that is, possessed at some times and not at others. A child develops to a point where she either has or has not acquired the requisite level of ability. A child, just like an adult, may nevertheless fail to display in *all* her decisions what she has acquired as a general ability.

What, then, are the elements of the ability that must be measured against the issue or decision? In the first place, this measure must be taken independently of any judgement of what is in the child's best interest. That a child would choose what is taken to be in her best interests is, at most, evidence that she does have sufficient intelligence and understanding of the relevant issue. Her making such a choice is not a necessary condition of her having the requisite ability. Similarly, the making by a child of a poor choice is not conclusive evidence of her general incapacity to choose for herself. Wise adults can occasionally make stupid decisions, just as fools sometimes get it right.

In the *Gillick* judgment Lord Scarman required of the child that she manifest an understanding of the 'nature' of the contraceptive advice offered and 'also have a sufficient maturity to understand what is involved' (*Gillick*, [1986] 189). We can distinguish here a number of possible elements. There is, first, knowledge of certain facts. A child, for instance, knows that a contraceptive acts to prevent conception that might otherwise result from sexual intercourse. Another child, by contrast, could simply be ignorant of, or unable to comprehend, the facts of reproduction. There is, second, an understanding of what follows *for the child* from an act or its omission. Thus failure to use a contraceptive could lead a young person who had sexual intercourse to become pregnant. These two understandings together constitute knowledge of the 'nature' of the act. Finally, there is what arguably comes with 'maturity' – the ability to appreciate the significance both of an act or its omission and of the relevant consequences. It is one thing to know what it is to become pregnant and another to understand what that means. This latter understanding involves realizing that pregnancy brings in its wake physical changes, that any resultant birth leaves a young person with a child to care for, and so on. Lord Scarman even insisted that the child would need to have an appreciation of the 'moral and family' questions involved.

Two interrelated responses can be, and have been, made to this requirement of competence. One is that it should surely be enough that a child understands the nature of the act (Williams, 1985). After all, no more is needed for an adult's consent than to be informed. In the law of contract adults need only to know what they are signing up to; they do not need a full appreciation of the contract's significance and of its import for their future lives. The second thing to say is that Gillick competence, as specified, is very demanding: there are many adults who, in making their choices, fail to display the maturity and 'understanding of what is involved' that is dictated as necessary for the child (Eekelaar, 1986a). Why, then, should a child have to display a competence that many adults lack both in general and in particular cases?

Summary

One important, indeed central, manner of understanding the moral status of the child is by questioning whether or not children have rights. It is normally thought that, according to the 'will' theory of rights, children cannot have rights, whereas according to the 'interest' theory they can. It is, however, at least possible on the 'will' theory that children could have rights, albeit ones that are exercised by trustees or representatives.

Child 'liberationists' claim that children have all the rights that adults do. Others deny this, either believing that children have no rights or believing that children have only some of the rights which adults possess. Those who believe children have no rights deny that children are qualified, as adults are, to have rights. They further argue that the ascription of rights to children manifests a misunderstanding of what children are like and of the nature of family relationships. Those who deny children all or some of the rights possessed by adults nevertheless believe that children, as human beings, have a certain moral status that ought to be protected.

Those who say that drawing a line between adults and children in respect of their possession of rights is arbitrary may mean different things. To deny that different capacities are progressively acquired at different ages is implausible. To insist that drawing a line as such is wrong ignores the point of doing so, and recourse to the alternative of a competency test is not appropriate or practicable. On the standard view, children have welfare but not liberty rights, whereas adults have both. Adults also have the right that their child-selves shall grow up to be adults of a certain sort. Children do not have an interest in remaining in childhood.

The best interest principle should have only limited application. It is not possible unambiguously to interpret the best interests of a child in terms of a hypothetical adult-self, and any objective interpretation will be the subject of contested views. A child's right to be heard in matters affecting her interests is a substitute for, not a complement to, the right of choosing for herself, and the Gillick competence which qualifies a child to exercise her rights of decision-making is stringently defined.

Chapter 2

The Family

Families Forever?

In this chapter I will examine the institution of the family and the rights of parents. I shall argue that, although it may be in a child's interest to be brought up within a family by parents, it is not clear that adults have rights over their own children. I shall expose an influential, but mistaken, view of natural parents as somehow the owners of those children they produce. I shall defend the view that parents have, rather than parental rights, duties to care for their children and discretion in their discharge. Finally, I shall consider what justice requires of families, both in their inner constitution and in their interrelationship.

Children are, for the very greatest part, raised within families and this seems always to have been the case. The family is one of the great, enduring institutions of organized human life. Indeed, it has persisted over history across extremely different kinds of society and culture. That does not mean that we cannot question whether or not children *should* be reared in families, and what is the most appropriate familial form for them to be raised within. Let me take each of these issues in turn.

Amy Gutman has helpfully contrasted the ideals of the 'family state' and of the 'state of families' (Gutman, 1987: ch. 1). According to the former ideal, it is the state that assumes the responsibility for the rearing of children whereas, according to the latter, it is families that are given this responsibility. Plato's *Republic* (Plato, 1941) is the most celebrated philosophical defence of a 'family state'. Strictly speaking, it was only in respect of that state's class of rulers that Plato commended collective rearing practices, and he did so for reasons of state rather than on account of any interests of the children. The abolition of the family secured the undivided loyalty of his favoured guardian class and permitted eugenic monitoring of that class's future quality.

It is probably fair to say that some form of the 'state of families' is the favoured standard within contemporary societies. That is not to deny that there have been experiments in collectivist rearing, but these have occurred at a substate level – that is, in small-scale communities, such as, notably, the Israeli *kibbutzim*, and, crucially, they have been voluntary. No state, since Plato's imagined ideal, has ever undertaken the project of collectively rearing all of its future citizens. Of course, the reasons why this is so are largely pragmatic, since the practical problems of publicly overseeing the upbringing of every child in a modern society are enormous and probably insuperable. But there are also important normative grounds for leaving families to look after children. What these are and how much discretion families have in the rearing of children will be considered in due course.

The rejection of the Platonic vision should not cause us to ignore at least two important considerations. First, it would be mistaken to view the 'family state' and the 'state of families' as the only two mutually exclusive alternatives. The latter ideal views the family as entrusted, and solely entrusted, with the care and nurture of children. Yet we can envisage various degrees of state monitoring of, and intervention in, the process of upbringing. At one extreme families are left entirely unsupervised and free to bring up children as they choose, and departures from this extreme will involve increasing elements of official control of this process. A favoured model within modern liberal democratic societies is that official intervention into family life is triggered only by a clear failure to provide a specified minimum level of care. Yet we can imagine more stringent standards, as well as more intrusive regulation, of familial life. In sum, collectivism with respect to the family comes in varying degrees.

The second consideration is that, even where the 'state of families' is the status quo and the generally favoured position, the family is not without its critics. Criticism of the family has come from a variety of sources. The anthropologist Edmund Leach, provoked outrage with his statement that '[f]ar from being the basis of the good society, the family, with its narrow privacy and tawdry secrets, is the source of all our discontents' (Leach, 1968: 44). More bluntly and directly, the poet Philip Larkin complained that parents 'fuck you up'. As the poem added, the parents were 'fucked up in their turn'. Thus 'Man hands on misery to man./ It deepens like a coastal shelf' (Larkin 'This Be The Verse' [1971] 1988: 180). These sentiments were expressed at a time when countercultural criticism focused on the family as a site of sexual repression, psychological dysfunction and narrow minded insularity. Indeed, a countercultural critic, such as the radical psychiatrist, R.D. Laing, felt able to attribute schizophrenia to the unendurable pressures of being brought up within traditional families (Laing, 1960, 1967).

More direct political criticism of the family has come from two important sources. First, feminists view the family as a locus of gender inequality and oppression, ranging from the perpetuation of traditional gender roles to the perpetration of domestic violence. Second, socialists have charged the family with being the instrument, in conjunction with the institution of private property, for the reproduction of structured socio-economic inequality. These criticisms raise the issues of, respectively, intrafamilial and interfamilial justice. Both will be further discussed in due course.

A response to the criticisms outlined above is that it is not the family that is at fault but rather particular familial forms or societies in which the family serves a particular function. This brings us to the question of the form of the family, for it is undoubtedly true that the family has changed its character from premodern to modern times. Some aspects of this change have been the subject of extended academic dispute. For instance, a once prevalent orthodoxy was that the modern nuclear family is to be contrasted with an extended premodern family whose membership spread beyond two generations and included servants, workers and others. This orthodoxy has been challenged, most notably by Peter Laslett (1963) who has been able to show that both family forms displayed roughly equal sizes. It is also an orthodoxy that children within premodern families were regarded with cold indifference and cruelly treated (Stone, 1977; de Mause, 1976). Yet there is clear evidence to the contrary (Pollock, 1983).

However, between premodernity and the present time there have been at least two changes in family form, broadly characterized, which are relevant to the present discussion. The first has been the shift from marriages founded on pragmatic or strategic considerations, such as the formation of an economic, familial or political alliance, to marriages based on love and mutual regard. This change represents the rise of the affective or 'sentimental' family (Okin, 1982). The second is the clearer separation of a public from a private realm. The distinction between public and private is an important one and it is particularly central to a modern liberal understanding of the proper extent of state intervention in the lives of citizens. It has also been associated with a contrast in the dispositions of, and relationships between, individuals. The line dividing the public and private has been drawn in different ways and in different places (Kymlicka, 2002: ch. 9, Section 2). Nevertheless, on one influential and paradigmatic view of the public–private divide, the family, and the domestic sphere, is a principal constituent of the private.

Whereas in premodern times the family was a public institution, in the modern era it is very much situated within the partially concealed and non-political domain of the private. The implications of these two changes for children are that they are now reared within families whose adult parties profess an affectionate commitment to one another, and whose life is, in the first instance, conducted outside the public world.

There is a further set of questions having to do with the form of the family, and these arise from consideration of the very basic question of what exactly counts as a family. It is probably impossible to supply a set of necessary and sufficient conditions that would serve to define any family – or, rather, any such conditions would need to be qualified with such words as 'typically' or 'normally'. I shall offer a stipulative and bare definition, before suggesting some further characteristics of paradigmatic families. Then I shall consider variations in the form. The bare definition is that a family is essentially a stable multigenerational association of adults and children serving the principal function of rearing its youthful members.

A family consists at least of some adults and some children. It need only comprise two generations, although it has not been uncommon for grandparents to live in the family home alongside the married child and her own children. It is stable in that the adult–children relationship is intended to be an enduring one. Adults who provide occasional, temporary foster care on a regular basis to the same children do not thereby constitute a family. A family normally shares a single habitation, although, again, it is not impossible that a family should be dispersed across more than one home. Familial relations are normally characterized by intimacy, affective closeness and unconditional love. Of course, not all families are happy ones, and, as Tolstoy famously observed, 'an unhappy family is unhappy after its own fashion' (Tolstoy, 1954: 13). When we speak of a normal family we should be careful to distinguish between what is statistically normal and what is commended as a norm. The traditional ideal of a family is one whose adult members form a married heterosexual couple.

What variations on this standard are possible? I shall indicate them without any accompanying evaluative comments. The adult couple within a family may be unmarried co-habitees. They may be homosexual. There may only be a single adult and this situation may have arisen from choice, or through separation, divorce or bereavement. According to the traditional ideal, again, the relationship between married adults and children should be a biological one – that is, the parents ought to rear their own children. But, once more, departures from this ideal are possible. The children may be adopted or, through remarriage of one of the partners, the children may be stepchildren.

Indeed, it is proper to note changes in family form that have occurred over the last 100 years and have become even more marked within the last 50 years. These changes mark a move away from the traditional familial form and can be noted without extended moral comment. In particular, four elements of these changes are important. The first is the rise of reproductive technology (with cloning even now appearing on the horizon). This has made it possible for those who would previously have been childless couples to have children. It has also made dramatically real the contingency of the relationship between what I will call 'causal' and 'custodial' parenthood. A causal parent is someone causally responsible for bringing a child into existence. A custodial parent is a person responsible, in significant part, for the upbringing of the child. The traditional ideal has been that of a married heterosexual couple procreating and raising their own offspring, but developments in reproductive technology now make it possible for several individuals to contribute to the creation of a child – the donor of semen, the donor of ova and the gestational mother. None of these needs to be one of the child's eventual custodial parents.

The rise of reproductive technology has also put considerable pressure on the idea of the family as a *natural* unit. We can distinguish between what is natural – how things are as a matter of their physical or biological constitution – and what is conventional – how they are as a matter of habit, custom, law or social arrangement. Is the family a natural or a conventional institution? In so far as parents have up until now been procreators, and vice versa, seemingly as a matter of physical necessity, it has been easy to see custodial parenthood as a natural, and inevitable, consequence of procreation. However, reproductive technology severs the automatic link between natural and custodial parenthood and also exposes the extent to which family arrangements are, and perhaps always have been, merely conventional artifices.

The second element in the changes in family form has been a greater tolerance of single-sex couples. In some jurisdictions this has been marked by official recognition of their unions, wich can mean according to these couples the same legal rights as are accorded to heterosexual marriages. Moreover, it may also mean allowing the parties of same-sex unions to have, or to acquire, parental responsibilities in respect of children that are identical to those enjoyed by parties to heterosexual marriages. The new reproductive technology also makes it that much easier for same-sex couples to have children.

The third element of these changes has been the decline of marriage which has been accompanied by a rise in the number of children born to cohabiting couples, a rise in divorce rates, and a consequent rise in the number of dependent children cared for by lone parents and by step-parents. In the United Kingdom, for instance, over one-third of all marriages are remarriages, one in five of all dependent children live in lone parent families, and one in four of all women aged between 18 and 49 are cohabiting.

The fourth element of the changes has been economic. With greater numbers of women included within the workforce, children are now more likely to have a working mother than would have been the case 50 years ago. This, in turn, has had implications for the traditional domestic division of labour between a male wage-earner and a woman confined to the management of the home.

These changes have meant that in most modern Western societies there are now a variety of familial forms. Only a proportion – and not always the majority – of these conform to the traditional ideal of a married heterosexual couple rearing their own offspring. Yet all of the possible variations still fit the basic stipulative definition offered above. This definition seeks to capture the essence of any family as an association of some adults and some children, and as having the function of supplying an upbringing to the children.

I listed some of the familial forms and indicated the main changes in them without offering any moral comment. However, it is important to note one kind of criticism of these variations in familial form, namely that some of the variant forms fail to serve the essential function of the family or serve it poorly. We can thus distinguish a 'functional' critique of a family form for failing to serve, or serving poorly, the proper function of the family, from a direct moral critique of a family form for being immoral (Galston, 1991: 280–81). The former argues that a certain kind of lifestyle and its consequent familial form is bad for the children it produces. The latter argues that the lifestyle is immoral. Thus it is one thing to criticize young single mothers for being feckless, sexually irresponsible individuals who are morally unsuited to rear their young, but it is another to view single parents as poorly placed to provide an adequate upbringing for their child. They are 'poorly placed' not because they are possessed of poor moral character but because of their impoverished social and economic circumstances and because children are always best brought up by two parents rather than one. Similarly, the practice of homosexuality may be morally condemned, and it may be said that their sexual identity morally disqualifies homosexuals from parenthood. But such criticism is distinct from the charge that single-sex couples cannot offer the gender role necessary for a proper upbringing of any children placed under their guardianship.

Whatever the familial form might be, why should we think that children are best brought up within a family? Reasons can be given from the side of the children, from that of the prospective parents, and that of the state and society. Let me briefly consider each in turn. Children need to be brought up. That is, they are essentially vulnerable, dependent beings who, at the early stage of human development, need dedicated care and nurture. Children do not simply grow up of their own accord and they cannot be left to their own devices. More positively, all the evidence shows that children benefit from being the object of the exclusive and committed care of some significant adults. Their physical and psychological health crucially depends on the possibility of such care.

From the side of adults, appeal will be made to a right to found a family. Such a right can be found in most international charters and conventions of human rights. For instance Article 12 of the European Convention on Human Rights guarantees that '[m]en and women of marriageable age have the right to marry and found a family, according to the national laws governing the exercise of this right' (Brownlie, 1993: 331). What such a right means and what might ground it will be considered shortly.

From the side of the state or of society in general there are several advantages. As has already been suggested, there are enormous practical problems in the state's assumption of the principal or exclusive custodial role. The state cannot be a parent to every one of its children, although, as we will see in Chapter 3, it can act as a guardian in the last instance.

There is also an important argument, based on liberal values, for the value to society of giving a principal role in the rearing of children to families (Blustein, 1982: 217–23). I shall call it the 'argument from pluralism' and it proceeds as follows. A central liberal value is that of individual autonomy or liberty – the freedom each person has to take and to exercise considered choices about how to lead her own life. In order to be able to exercise this liberty it is necessary that a person should have certain capacities – that, for instance, of being able to reflect upon and evaluate the options open to them. We might call this one of the internal preconditions of autonomy. But autonomy also has external conditions and chief amongst these is the existence of a range of feasible and valuable lifestyles from which each of us can choose. This need not be a large range. Furthermore, the individual facing only one life prospect might be said to choose it autonomously if it is one that she endorses – that is, one which she would choose in preference to alternatives. Thus, even if we are already committed to a particular manner of leading our own life, it is important that we should be able to test our commitment against alternatives. In short, we need a pluralistic culture in which we are exposed to a number of different ways of life.

We might also emphasize a further internal condition of autonomy. This is the possession by each individual of a set of values and beliefs – an outlook on life. The individual certainly need not retain this outlook throughout his whole life: valuing autonomy leads to the idea that each person should subject his core ideas and ideals to rational reflection, subsequently endorsing, modifying or rejecting them. The values we live by, if we are autonomous, are those we have scrutinized and found acceptable. Yet autonomy is not exercised in a vacuum. In choosing who it is we want to be, we must start from somewhere. Each of must at least have an initial outlook on life, even if it is not the one we subsequently retain unaltered.

But, having specified these internal and external conditions of autonomy, what could be more evident than the role the family can play in providing them? Given that each of us is brought up in a family, each of us acquires a distinctive and very particular set of beliefs and values – an outlook on life that we owe to our parents' own convictions and the manner in which they chose to share these with us. Each family is different in its own particular way and so too is the product of each familial upbringing. Thus a state of families sustains a pluralistic culture and, at the same time, ensures that each child grows up with a distinctive and substantive outlook on life.

It is relatively easy to see how a family state, by comparison, would be incapable of reproducing such diversity. Indeed, advocates of collectivist modes of child-rearing have favoured them largely because they secure conformity in the outcomes of upbringing. Those who want their community's citizens to think similarly could not trust to families to bring up its children. A state can only have civic uniformity if it assumes the responsibilities of guardianship.

The 'argument from pluralism' is an important one and we will return again to some of the issues raised by it. However, even at this stage, it is necessary to be clear that, within the argument, it is the ideal of autonomy not that of pluralism which is doing the real evaluative work. A pluralistic culture is important not for its own sake but because it is the natural outcome of the exercise of autonomous life-choices and, at the same time, the invaluable, indeed indispensable, background against which autonomy is exercised. This point is significant for it means that children must still be reared to be autonomous. If all that mattered was pluralism as such it would suffice that families produced heteronomous adults with very different outlooks on life. What the argument from pluralism shows, however, is that families are to be valued for producing diverse, but also autonomous, adults.

The Right to Found a Family?

We have given reasons why families, in various possible forms, might be thought valuable – for children and for society at large. What argument can be made on behalf of prospective parents? Is there a moral right, corresponding to the existing international legal right, to found a family? And what exactly does such a right amount to? Having a family consists in having and in rearing children. I have stipulatively defined a family as an association of adults and children having the principal function of bringing up the latter. In due course I will examine what rights, if any, adults have over those children who might be entrusted to their care. First, I want to consider how a possible association of adults and children comes about. What gives an adult human being a right to stand in a certain initial custodial relationship to a child or children? We normally understand founding a family as comprising both bringing children into being and occupying, in the first instance, the relationship to them of presumptive guardian. Of course, the individual who becomes the custodial parent of a child who is not her own – someone who adopts or provides long-term foster care for a child – also founds a family, but I am interested, primarily, in the double, and seemingly interrelated, actions of having – that is, producing – and rearing children.

The right to have children is not a positive simple correlate of a putative right not to have them, as some have argued (Robertson, 1983). Although the use of a single term, 'procreative liberty', to denote a freedom to choose whether or not to have offspring suggests otherwise, we should not see the right not to have children as simply one side of a coin whose obverse side is the right to have children. We might grant that adults should have the normative power to determine that they will not procreate, and such a power underpins rights to contraception and, more controversially, to abortion. However, these rights are best understood as rights of control over one's own body and its fertility. They are rights that govern what happens to one's own person. The alleged right to have children is a right to bring into existence another human being. It is thus a right governing what shall happen to someone else – namely, a possible future person. It is also true that procreation affects others indirectly inasmuch as the addition of another human being in a shared world makes some difference to the lives of others.

However, even if there is a right to reproduce, it is at most a negative liberty right – a right whose exercise should not be prevented or interfered with – rather than a positive right to the provision of the means necessary for the performance of the activity. The thought on negative rights is as follows. If there is something I rightfully could and would otherwise do, I should not be stopped from doing it. But it does not follow from this that I am entitled to help in doing what I could not otherwise do. This is so even if it is something I want to do and would choose to do if I could.

For instance, if I have a negative liberty right of emigration, I have a right to unobstructed departure from my country. The state should not, other things being equal, stop me from leaving if I want to. But such a right is not a positive right to assisted passage. It does not oblige the state to provide me with the means whereby I can emigrate. The right of free movement is the right to officially unobstructed travel, not the right of travel at no cost to the traveller. So, in similar terms, a negative right of reproductive freedom is the right to have children if one is able to. The state is obliged not to render the individual infertile – by compulsory sterilization, for instance – and not to interfere with the natural course of any chosen pregnancy – by involuntary abortion, for instance. The negative right of reproduction is not a positive right to assisted reproduction.

This is not to say that the infertile might not have a warranted claim against the state for the provision of fertility treatment. They might do so on the grounds that their infertility is the cause of serious mental distress that is more effectively dealt with by treating the infertility than by psychiatric therapy for the depression (Singer and Wells, 1984). Alternatively, they might claim that their infertility is a handicap which liberal principles of equality prescribe should be compensated for by the provision of state-funded fertility treatment (Burley, 1998). These claims cannot be assessed here, as all that is necessary is to note that a right to have children is *not* a right to be assisted in the production of children. Equally, it is obviously not a right to be given other people's children if one is unable to have them oneself. If there were such a right, the state would be under an obligation to redistribute children from the successfully fertile to the infertile, and our collective judgement that this would be unfair (rather than simply harmful to the children) is, I suspect, a settled and strong conviction. Nevertheless it is an interesting proposition in the following respect. Liberal egalitarianism is arguably informed by the core principle that individuals should be compensated for the effects of their brute bad luck (Cohen, G.A., 1989). However, acting on this principle is also arguably constrained by a principle of self-ownership. We have a legitimate title to our selves and to our bodies. It thus would not be appropriate to compensate a sightless person for their unchosen bad fortune by transplanting (if it could be done) an eye from a healthy person (G.A. Cohen, 1995: 70). Why not? Because, although it is my good luck to have two good eyes, and your bad luck to have none, these are *my* eyes. Can the fertile person similarly claim that her child is *hers* and thus not up for possible grabs? Later, I will give reasons to doubt that a natural parent's claim over her child does derive from a principle of self-ownership.

What grounds a right to have children? Adults can want children for a whole variety of reasons, some of which can be, and are, highly morally dubious. Nevertheless, it is undoubtedly true that having children engages some of the deepest and most central values in a person's life. It also seems true that what matters most to people is having their *own* children. Whilst very many infertile couples might be more than happy to adopt a child, it is clear that the vast majority would prefer not to be infertile. The desire of an adult to have her own child is inseparably bound up with that adult's understanding of what gives her own life significance and value. This desire is thus an extremely powerful one and yet it need not be a selfish one. What kinds of good reason can be given for having children?

One set of reasons has to do with the idea of playing one's part in the creation of something that has value. The value in question both derives from one's own person and yet, at the same time, transcends and outlives one's own contribution. To bring into the world a human being is to create something that is original and that is itself the source of new value. A second set of good reasons for having children has to do with the role that a child born to a couple may play in making objective, or concrete, the sexual love between them. Hegel, in obscure if concise terms, argued that it is only with the birth of offspring that conjugal love becomes a 'knowing that knows' (quoted in Honneth, 1995: 39). This set of reasons will not, however, persuade those who consider that the value to a couple of their sexual love is quite distinct from the value to them of having children and it moreover presupposes a dubious view of love as something externalized or realized in the production of new human beings. Finally, there are reasons to have children of one's own that have to do with the quality of the ensuing parent–child relationship. A natural parent rearing her own child knows that child more deeply, cares more for her, and is better motivated to do the best for that child than she would if the child were not her own.

If, then, there are good reasons for having a child, are there equally good reasons not to have a child? Clearly, it would be a reason not to have a child if it were better for the child not to be born. There are much debated philosophical difficulties in making sense of this claim. For example, can a non-existent person complain about not having been brought into existence? But let us assume that we can understand what is meant. An adult's right to have a child of her own is surely outweighed by the right of a possible person not to be born into a life that is not worth living. Thus, for instance, prospective parents should not bring into existence a severely handicapped child if they can avoid doing so (Harris, 1989). Others besides the parent and child are also affected by the creation of a new human being. In so far as we must all share a finite world with scarce resources, an additional claimant on these resources makes a material difference to everyone else's life prospects.

These considerations – which will be discussed further later on – do not demonstrate that an adult has no right to have children, but they do show that any such right is arguably constrained by at least two putative duties. One is the duty to ensure that the child whom one plays one's part in creating may reasonably be expected to have a life that is worth living. The second is a duty to ensure that the creation of an extra human being does not, directly or indirectly, significantly worsen the lives of anyone else. I will further discuss these constraints when examining the nature and limits of any parental rights over children.

Let us grant, then, that adults have a right to bring a child into existence, subject to the constraints indicated, if they are able to. This is not yet a right to found a family for, as indicated at the beginning of this section, such a right also encompasses a right to stand in the relationship of presumptive guardian to any child brought into existence. Why should I be entitled to bring up whomsoever I create? There need be no general presumption in favour of the right of each adult to act as a parent – that is, to be a guardian as such. Indeed, some think parenting may be viewed as belonging to a class of activities which have potentially harmful consequences for others and require the possession of a minimal level of relevant skills and abilities if these harms are to be avoided. This class of activities – into which performing surgery and driving a car also fall – is elsewhere regulated by the issuing of licences to practise. Why should it be any different with parenting? Why should parents not be licensed (LaFollette, 1980)?

This proposal is beset by problems and is also open to principled criticism (Frisch, 1981). It is not clear that being a parent is strictly and exactly analogous to surgery or car-driving. Both these latter activities are attended throughout by significant risks of serious injury which can be substantially reduced by the acquisition of determinate and testable skills. Is parenting risky in the same way? What, moreover, could be agreed to be the necessary level of demonstrable parenting skill that would serve as the qualification for possession of a parental licence? As was pointed out in Chapter 1, it is very difficult to agree on what counts as a good parenting. Even if the requirement was simply for *good enough* parenting, it is still far from obvious what could be agreed as showing, in advance of the parenting, evidence of the skills needed to be capable only of that.

Any licensing scheme needs to be fairly and efficiently administered. Could this be guaranteed in the case of a parental licence? Much is at stake. Those desperate to have children would often break or bend laws, and seek to bribe officials, in the pursuit of this goal. Enormous pressure would be put on the administrators of a parental licensing scheme. The scheme would require the successful identification of everyone about to have a child. It would need a method of removing children from unlicensed parents. It would require a scheme of punishing those unlicensed parents who continue to procreate or who seek to evade detection.

Finally, it may be that children could be as effectively protected by a less objectionable and more efficacious scheme of child protection. Removing children from seriously abusive parents, and providing them with alternative carers, is, in effect, to deny the original parents, after the fact, a licence to rear their children. Nevertheless, for all its faults, the argument for a system of parental licensing serves dramatically to illustrate the dangers of readily assuming that we all should be allowed to act as parents just because we are adult human beings.

Returning to the particular question of whether an individual should be allowed to act as a parent of a child she has created, two distinctions prove useful. The first is between a causal parent and a custodial parent. As indicated earlier, I mean by the former an adult who is in some part causally responsible for a child coming into existence. This may, for instance, be through the donation of sperm or of ova or it may be by playing a gestational role as is done by the surrogate mother who carries to term the implanted fertilized ovum of two other causal parents. By a custodial parent I mean an adult accorded a role in the caring for, and rearing of, a child. We may further distinguish between *de jure* and *de facto* custodial parents. The former are those adults who, by law, custom or social rule are formally accorded the rights and responsibilities of parenthood in respect of a child. The latter are those who as a matter of fact actually undertake these responsibilities and assume the exercise of these rights.

The second distinction that can be usefully made is between the right to be a parent and the rights of a parent. The right to be a parent is the right to stand to a specific child in the relationship of parent. The rights of a parent are the rights of custodianship over that child which help to specify that relationship. Strictly speaking, there is no distinction to be made here since the right to be a parent just is the right to exercise the custodial powers of a parent. However the distinction, even if artificially made, serves to focus attention on two distinct questions. First, what is it that entitles one to be a parent? Second, what is it to be a parent? One very influential account of parenthood, the proprietarian, which will be examined in due course, provides a ready answer to each question. One is entitled to be a parent because one is the producer, and thereby the owner, of one's child. Since a parent owns a child, her rights in respect of the child are those of an owner.

However, it is possible to find an answer to the first question, 'What entitles one to be a parent?', without prejudging the second question of what, normatively, is involved in being a parent – that is, without specifying what is entailed by custodial parenthood. Moreover, one very obvious, and hugely influential, answer to the first question is that one is a causal parent – that is, one is entitled to exercise custodianship over what one has causally brought into existence. This view can be maintained without subscribing to the proprietarian theory that parents own what they produce. Instead, it can be supported by the idea that producing a child means that one stands in a special and unique relationship to the child – a relationship that has both its own character and putative implications for the quality of the upbringing that can be offered. The presumption that natural – that is, causal – parents should be allowed to care for their own children is the predominant understanding of parenthood in modern society.

Let me critically review some reasons for considering this presumption to be well grounded. In such a review one needs carefully to distinguish reasons from the side of the child and reasons from the side of the prospective parent. That is, it may be in a child's best interests to be brought up by her natural parents, but that is different from saying that, independently of how it goes for the child, a natural parent can lay claim to be the guardian of her own offspring. On the side, then, of the child are the following reasons. First, natural parents are the best suited to care for their own children. Biology disposes them to give love to their offspring – a love that is often unconditional and self-sacrificial. John Locke, for instance, believed that God had 'in all the parts of the Creation taken a peculiar care to propagate and continue the several species of Creatures, and make the Individuals act so strongly to this end that they sometimes neglect their own private good for it' (Locke, 1963: I, Chapter VI, § 56). The behaviour of human beings as caring natural parents is consistent with that of most other parents in the animal kingdom. Of course, this is not universally true. Some natural parents are cruel, abusive and neglectful. However, these are exceptions to the general rule that may normally, and with good reason, be relied upon.

Second, being raised by one's own natural parents contributes appropriately to the identity and self-image of the maturing child. The healthy development of any person requires the successful acquisition of a positive and stable self-image. The fact that the child and parent share heredity and, in consequence, are significantly alike in respect of appearance, skill and general abilities greatly facilitates this. In turn, such mutual identification makes possible and fosters the deep, reciprocated affection that characterizes the best parent–child relations. Again, this is not to deny that adults have happily and successfully reared children who were not their own, nor that very many who know themselves to have been adopted make no effort retrospectively to discover their natural parents.

Third, allowing for natural parents to care for their own children solves a coordination problem in that it is best that *some* arrangement is generally agreed upon although there is no reason to prefer one particular arrangement, as such, over another. Thus it is best if everyone within a well-defined road system drives on the same side of the road, but there is no reason to think that driving on the left as such is better or worse than driving on the right. Similarly, it is best if there is some system for the allocation of children to parents. Specific adults must have, and know that they have, a responsibility to care for specific children. As we noted earlier, children need to be brought up and, more particularly, benefit from being the object of the exclusive and committed care of some significant adults. If the duty to care for children were left merely as a duty for all or for anyone to discharge, then some, perhaps very many, children would not be cared for at all. Coordination problems can be solved if there is some salient fact that all can recognize and that, further, suggests a generally agreeable arrangement. The fact of natural parenthood is such a salient fact.

There are, then, good reasons for causal parents to assume the roles of custodial parents. However, the following qualifications should be entered. First, none of these reasons appeals to the idea that the mere fact of being of a natural parent is somehow sufficient to ground a claim to custodial parenthood. There is, in this sense, nothing about natural parenthood as such which shows a natural parent to be a good, least of all the best, parent. Second, the reasons offered all rest on the interests of the child. It is better, so the various arguments considered suggest, for the child if her natural parents raise her. No reason has been given as to why a natural parent has a reason, simply in virtue of being a natural parent, to raise her own children. Indeed, it is not clear what these reasons might be (Archard, 1995).

Third, if the balance of reasons does indicate that causal parents should be custodial parents, this is only a defeasible presumption in their favour. When particular causal parents show themselves to be poor parents, incapable of properly caring for their own offspring, they can make no claim against any loss of custodial rights by appeal to the fact of being the child's natural parents. Fourth, we should remember that one and the same child may have three causal parents. Moreover, these various adults may make competing and conflicting claims to custody over that child. To agree that causal parents can make a claim to be custodial parents is not to agree how we should resolve such disputes. It would certainly be mistaken to argue along the lines that one causal parent made a greater causal contribution to the creation of the child than another and is thus entitled to a greater say in the care of the child.

The Proprietarian Argument

As already stated, the proprietarian account of parenthood is highly influential and it continues to cast a long shadow over the way in which we think about the relationship between a parent and child. It provides an answer to the questions of who may be a custodial parent and of what custody consists in. The answer in both cases is given in terms of ownership and property. The proprietarian argument has its roots in a celebrated defence of private property by John Locke (Locke, 1963: I, Chapter V) and the entire argument, including the more general defence, is worth spelling out formally.

Note that this is an argument for the *original* acquisition of property; the question of the warranted transfer to others of what has been originally acquired is a separate one.

1 Every person has a right to own his person.
2 Therefore, every person has a right to own the labour of his person.
3 Therefore, every person has a right to own that with which he has mixed his labour (the 'fruits of his labour').
4 Sexual reproduction is an instance of 'mixing' one's labour.
5 Therefore, a causal parent is entitled to own what is the fruit of one's reproductive labour, namely the child.

(1) to (3) represent the general defence of private property (Day, 1966: 208), whilst the further premises (4) and (5) represent the specific application of that defence to the outcome of reproductive labour. In essence, the argument maintains that we are entitled to own what we produce and since parents produce children, they are their legitimate proprietors.

Before proceeding to evaluate this argument we should note that its conclusion was infamously once instantiated in Roman law. According to the doctrine of *patria potestas* a parent – more particularly, the father as head of the family, the *paterfamilias* – had the unfettered power of life and death over his children. A father could thus dispose of his children as property or kill them as he saw fit. Interestingly, the power was transitive so that both father and son remained within the *potestas* of a living grandfather. Further, the power was exercised at the same time as sons, under public law, had the rights to vote and to hold office. Nevertheless, although the doctrine fell into desuetude in the later period of the Roman Empire, it did strictly mean that the state of being the property of one's *paterfamilias* ended only with death or formal emancipation (Nicholas, 1962: 65–68; Lacey, 1986; Boswell, 1988: 58–75; MacKenzie 1862: Chapter IX).

How, then, are we to evaluate the proprietarian argument? We should note, first, that there are general criticisms of steps (1) to (3) of the argument – that is, the defence of private property. Can a person be said to own herself? Kant thought it impossible to be both a person and a thing, 'the proprietor and the property' (Kant, 1963: 165). Locke himself disallowed slavery and suicide, both of which should be permissible if we can own ourselves. Many, however, consider the ideal of self-ownership not only plausible but foundational. At its most basic, individuals surely have some moral title over their own bodies and their own powers.

What of conclusion (3)? Are we entitled to the fruits of our labour? Locke's own account in terms of a 'mixing' of one's labour has been subjected to extensive criticism (Nozick, 1974: 174–78). If labour does ground an entitlement, it is surely not in consequence of the mere fact of admixture, but rather of the fact that effort has been expended at a cost to the labourer or that additional value has been created through the labouring. It is, of course, still a further moot point whether these facts ground an entitlement to full ownership rights in what has been laboured on, rather than simply an income in compensation for the expended effort or remuneration for the creation of extra value. There are still further difficulties raised by cooperative labour and by successive production processes involving different labourers.

However, let us leave these difficulties to one side. If some version of a general argument for private property through labour is defensible, what follows for the production of children? In other words, let us grant that individuals are self-owning and that they own the fruits of their labour. Quite obviously, not only pregnancy but the whole business of caring for and rearing a child to maturity is a time-consuming, exhausting, demanding and occasionally painful expenditure of labour which creates something of undoubted value, another human being. Why, then, is a child not the fruit of her parents' labours and thus their rightful property?

It will not do simply to assert that children are human beings and not the sort of things that can be owned. This is simply to beg the question against the argument. It will also not do to point out the paradoxical implications of the argument. Since each of us was once a child and thus the fruit of our parents' labours, each of us is owned by our parents. But since our parents were also once children they were, or still are, owned by *their* parents. And so on back to the original parent, the primogenitor of all humanity. However, since what is owned by others cannot own herself, no human, save the first, is self-owning, and hence no claims to own one's children can be generated for any human being bar possibly one. This paradox was identified by Sir Robert Filmer who was the object of Locke's criticisms in the first of his Treatises of Government. Filmer simply followed the Old Testament in seeing Adam as the primogenitor of all subsequent humanity and as given sovereign dominion by God. Subsequently everything is owned by Adam's successors, the succession being determined by a primogenital principle (Steiner, 1994: 242–43).

Locke's own two efforts to avoid the unpalatable implications of his own proprietarian argument are inadequate. The first argument proceeds as follows (Locke, 1963: I, Chapter I, §52–54). One does not own what one does not deliberately and knowingly design. As the process of sexual reproduction is opaque to those who engage in it, one does not own children. But many creative processes are, in this sense, opaque to the creator. Moreover, the development of reproductive science has simply rendered the process in question increasingly transparent. The second argument (Locke, 1963: I, Chapter I, § 54) is that God is ultimately the author of His children. But, then, it is surely true that God is the author, in the final analysis, of *all* things. That would make humans at most trustees but not owners of *whatever* they themselves produce.

The contemporary neo-Lockean, Hillel Steiner, blocks the unpalatable conclusion by arguing that children are *not* fully the fruit of their parents' labour since they require natural resources in the form of genetic information transmitted from previous generations (Steiner, 1994: 248). Of course, that might only imply that parents should be taxed for the use of these resources. It need not show that parents have *no* proprietorial claim on the fruits of their progenitive labour. Others have argued that the entitlement to own the fruits of one's labours derives from the more fundamental entitlement to own one's own person. Since one cannot own what is itself self-owning and inasmuch as a child is, or at least becomes, self-owning it cannot thus be owned by its parents (Becker, 1977: 38–39). This argument does not beg the question by simply asserting that humans cannot be owned. Rather, it tries to show that any claim to ownership of *anything* presupposes self-ownership which thereby constrains the limits of legitimate ownership. It is only because we human beings are self-owning that we can own anything; therefore we cannot own another human being.

The Extension Claim

These counterarguments may or may not succeed. The fact remains that the proprietarian argument is highly influential. Whilst it is repugnant to think of children as owned by their parents, nevertheless, as many comment, there are features of the parent–child relationship which prompt a proprietorial explanation (Bigelow *et al.*,

1988: 183). In the modern period few, if any, are prepared openly to defend the view that children are their parents' property. The libertarian, Jan Narveson, *does* think parents have property rights over their offspring but argues that these are severely constrained by a public interest in the welfare and effect on others of the future adults these children will become (Narveson, 1998: 272–74). Barbara Hall (1999) has argued for a version of Locke's argument, but would substitute for (4) in the argument above a claim to the effect that parents own their genetic material, and a suitably modified conclusion follows. This is noteworthy. As we have seen, Steiner appeals to the fact that the parents do *not* own all the genetic material that goes into making up a child in order to block the unpalatable conclusion of the Lockean argument. Edgar Page (1984) defends a quasi-proprietarian argument to the effect that parents have a very great interest in having, and in shaping, a child of their own. An interest of this sort reflects the property rights people have in certain kinds of object.

One attempt to capture what is special about the parent–child relationship, but one that falls short of a proprietorial claim can be called the 'extension' claim. An early version of it is to be found in Aristotle. He compares the sovereignty of a man over his chattels to that of a father over his child and concludes that a child 'until it reaches a certain age and sets up for itself' is 'as it were part of himself' – that is, the parent (Aristotle, 1984: V, Chapter 6, 1134b). Some contemporary philosophers have similarly been happy to characterize children if not as exactly things to be owned, then certainly as mere extensions of their parents. Robert Nozick, for instance, describes children as 'part of one's substance . . . part of a wider identity you have' (Nozick, 1989: 28). Charles Fried also writes that 'the right to form one's child's values, one's child's life plan and the right to lavish attention on the child are extensions of the basic right not to be interfered with in doing those things for oneself' (Fried, 1978: 152).

The extension claim does not view the child as being literally an extension of its parents. Aristotle's 'as it were' qualifies the claim. The child is an extension of her parent in that what the parent chooses for his own life involves also choosing for his child. Choosing for his child is an extension of his own choices. It should be noted that the language of Nozick and Fried obscures the fact that there may be several parents. The 'one' of whom the child is an extension need not be single. Nor need the parents make the same choices for *their* 'extended' selves (Macleod, 1997: 138, fn 14).

The extension claim gives plausible expression to a widely shared sense that having and bringing up one's own child gives a broader shape to a parent's sense of herself. It may swallow up an adult's whole life, lending it a purpose and meaning it might otherwise not have. Indeed, a parent may sincerely claim that having a child defines what she is to the exclusion of almost everything else in her life. All of this may be true. But why should it ground parental rights? There are many things that could be plausibly described as giving 'substance' to one's life, as forming part of one's 'wider identity'. These include, amongst other things, an enduring close friendship, service to an institution or company, support for one's sports team and membership of an association or group. Why, by analogy, should not one's rights of choice with respect to one's own life extend over one's close friend, fellow employees, the sports team and fellow group members? The fact is that one does not think of a person as having such an extended right in these kinds of case. But this then casts doubt on the extension claim in respect of parents and their child. Or it suggests that this claim is really only a disguised version of a proprietarian claim. For what may really be meant by saying that a child is an extension of her parent is just that the parent owns the child.

There is a weaker version of the extension claim that might be called 'the shared life claim'. This does not show that parents have rights over their children, but it does show that what a child will do within a family is a function of the choices adults make for the family as a whole. The claim goes as follows. Grant that individuals do have a right to have children, and to join with other adults in order to share the task of rearing these children. The family which is created in this fashion will most likely be a small group engaged in a range of conjoint activities – sharing the same living space, eating, going on holiday, relaxing and playing together. Standardly, these shared activities will take place in comparative privacy, unobserved and unregulated by other adults.

Characteristic of family life is its intimacy, that is its closeness and emotional openness. Family members normally love and trust one another. This love motivates and is reinforced by the intimacy and shared life. Such a picture of family life is an admittedly idealized one. It is intended to provide an account of the most propitious circumstances in which, in consequence of sharing a life, children will come to share an outlook on life. For it is highly probable that, in such circumstances, children will adopt the way of life, broadly characterized, which they have shared with their parents. They will inherit many of their parents' core beliefs and values. This will be motivated by their identification with their parents and by the particular context the family represents for acquiring an outlook on life.

When a child chooses to value what his parents value this is not simply because the parents' choices for their children are an extension of their own choices. Rather, it derives from sharing a family life. For example, according to the extension claim, a parent's right to form her child's religious views is merely an extension of her right to practise the religion of her own choice. The 'shared life claim', on the other hand, acknowledges that an important part of a family's shared activities might be religious observance. The parent does not choose for the child who, on the contrary, may or may not choose to participate in this shared activity. If the child does profess her parents' religious beliefs, this may be a consequence of sharing their life. On the 'shared life' view parents do not have a right to choose a religion for their children. On the 'extension' view they do.

Parental Rights or Parental Duties?

If no foundation for parental rights can be found in a proprietarian argument or in some version of the extension claim, do parents have any rights over their children? One influential claim is that any rights that parents do have are constrained by, and derive from, a prior duty to care for their children. Kant thought that parents having brought a child into being thereby 'incur an obligation to make the child content with his condition as far as they can'. Further, 'from this duty there must necessarily also arise the right of parents to *manage* and develop the child' (Kant, 1996: 64–65). This is an early version of the 'priority thesis' (Blustein, 1982: 104–14) which states that parents have, in the first instance, duties to do certain things for their children. What these duties might be we will examine shortly. We can also grant that parents have duties not to all children in general, but rather to specific children. Indeed, we can grant that primary responsibility for the care of a child should, initially at least, be assigned to the adults whose relationship to the child is a salient one, such as, most obviously, her causal parents.

What parental rights does the priority thesis accord to parents? Essentially, they are rights to exercise a degree of autonomous choice in the rearing of a child but subject to the discharge of the duty of care. In other words, parents can decide what a child should eat, read, watch on TV, what time they should go to bed, what is proper punishment for bad behaviour and so on, so long as these decisions are made in fulfilment of the duty of care. On this account, parents can have no parental rights other than those allowed for by, and following from, the discharge of this duty. Moreover, there can be no conflict between the parents' rights and their duties in respect of their children since all of these rights derive from the antecedent duty.

Is the priority thesis persuasive? There are two very different kinds of rejoinder to it. One is that the rights parents claim to have are not exhaustively specified by those that follow from the duty of care. For instance, a parent's right to choose his child's religion does not seem to derive from any duty of care (Page, 1984: 188), and such a right is recognized in many charters. However, one could, of course, simply deny that there should be any such right. What exists in law need not be a well-grounded moral right.

The second rejoinder is that the rights which are argued to be based in a parental duty of care are not rights proper at all. Certainly, parents have some degree of discretion as to how they choose to discharge this duty, but they have no discretion as to whether or not they do discharge it (Montague, 2000). Compare the case where there is a statutorily enforced obligation to vote in national elections. A citizen can choose how to cast his vote – that is, decide which candidate or candidates will be marked as preferred – but she does not have a choice as to whether or not to vote. Yet a right to vote *is* the liberty to vote or to abstain from voting.

Perhaps this example is misleading. After all, an Australian can cast her vote (even if legally she must) whilst a merely temporary visitor to that country cannot. Consider also the following example. A property-owner is legally ordered to equip her property with adequate security measures. She has no choice but to do so. In respect of whether or not she provides security she lacks a liberty right. But, so long as the security she provides is adequate, she does have a choice as to the form it takes. If she builds a perimeter wall, for instance, she can determine what materials it is made of. She can also decide what level of security beyond the specified level of adequacy she will put in place. Finally, it is her property and her security. Others are duty-bound not to interfere with the measures she takes to make the property secure and to respect the title she has to the property.

It is easy enough to think of the parent who is duty-bound to provide a certain level of care for her child in analogous terms. How she provides that care is down to her, care beyond the specified threshold is discretionary, and it is *her* child she cares for. Even if it is inappropriate to describe the child as her property, nevertheless others are under an obligation not to interfere with, or obstruct, her in her performance of her care-giving role.

Would it be better, then, to speak of parental autonomy or parental discretion in the discharge of the duty of care? The obvious danger in speaking only of parental duties is that we thereby think of the parent as merely an agent of the child's welfare. Yet a parent also has interests, and these are bound up with the activity of parenting. Being a parent is extremely important to a person. Even if the child is not to be thought of as the property or even as an extension of the parent, the shared life of a parent and child involves an adult's purposes and aims at the deepest level. In consequence, no moral theory of parenthood should interpret 'the parent's role in ways that make individual parents no more than instruments of their children's good' (Callan, 1997: 144–45).

This is not just to say that an adequate moral theory of parenthood must impartially treat the interests of both parent and child. Any adequate moral theory must treat impartially the interests of *all* affected parties. It would therefore be wrong to deny that parents have interests that should count: parents have an interest *in parenting* – that is, in sharing a life with, and directing the development of, their child. It is not enough not to discount the interest of parents in a moral theory of parenthood. What must also merit full and proper consideration is the interest of someone in being a parent. That is why it is important to understand, and evaluate, the different reasons adults have for becoming parents.

What does the parental duty of care require of a parent? In the first instance, a parent must be paternalist – that is, make, for the child, those choices that promote her interests but which that child is incapable of making for herself. The parent may make these choices until the child is mature enough to make her own choices. At the point at which the child has herself become an adult the parent's duty of care is fulfilled. Indeed, the exercise of parental paternalism may be gradually diminished as the child matures. John Locke gave elegant expression to this idea. As children 'grow up to the use of reason,' 'the rigour of government' may be 'gently relaxed' (Locke, 1960: § 41). Of course, that is not to say that a parent should not continue to love and be concerned for her offspring after they reach the age of majority, but she is under no obligation to care for them.

It is probably fair to observe that the paternalist and the proprietarian accounts provide the principal, and competing, justifications for the exercise of parental authority over children (Montgomery, 1988). Thomas Murray objects to the stark alternatives given for modelling the parent–child relationship of proprietarianism and 'stewardship' – that is, the parent's paternalist caretaking of the child. In proprietarianism the child is nothing but the property or extension of the parent. In stewardship the parent is seemingly nothing but the agent of the child's good. Murray suggests 'mutualism' as a proper model of the parent–child relationship. This is a model which emphasises 'the central importance of the *relationship*, without losing sight of the individuality of the parties' (Murray, 1996: 61). According to mutualism, the good of parent and child are intertwined, the parent deriving benefits from her promotion of the child's flourishing.

I have already noted that a parent's interest in parenting should be properly acknowledged and that being a parent connects at the most profound level with a person's sense of herself. A parent is not just a means to the child's good. It is also true that parent–child relationships at their best are characterized by loving mutuality, joint participation in shared lives of intense affection wherein each party's good is inseparably bound up with that of the other. However, mutualism does not answer the normative question, 'Why may parents choose for their children?' It is undoubtedly the case that a loving parent can choose for her child in the spirit of mutuality. In this, she is not a selfless promoter of the child's good with no sense of her own; she enjoys a shared life with her child. Nevertheless, she does choose *for* her child. The shared life of parent and child is not one that each independently chooses for herself. Even if what the parent chooses for the child benefits both parent and child – and there is always the danger of merely paying lip-service to the child's good when it is the parent who benefits – the choice on behalf of the child needs a warrant.

What, then, justifies this parental paternalism? Thomas Hobbes believed that children are in 'absolute subjection' to parents who may 'alienate them . . . pawn them for hostages, kill them for rebellion, or sacrifice them for peace' (Hobbes, 1994: 23.8). Yet he also thought that this dominion did not derive from generation – that is, the fact of causing the child to come into being. Rather, it comes 'from the Child's Consent, either expresse, or by other sufficient arguments declared' (Hobbes, 1968: Part II, Chapter 20). Some, more liberal than Hobbes, seek for a justification of paternalism in the retrospective agreement somebody would give to having been treated paternalistically (Carter, 1977). Others explicitly sanction paternalism towards children by means of the idea of future-oriented consent (Dworkin, 1971: 119).

However, there are real difficulties in an appeal to the idea of consent in this context. Many children, on leaving their families, explicitly reject the upbringing they received, but this does not show that the parents acted impermissibly when they raised the child. A child might never grow up, dying before reaching her majority. Yet counterfactual appeals – in this instance, to the consent she *would* have given – are notoriously difficult to confirm or deny. It is better, then, to say the following. A child cannot act independently to promote her own good, so an adult is warranted in acting on behalf of the child to promote her good. A parent is thus a 'steward' (Brennan and Noggle, 1997: 11), or a 'trustee' (Beck *et al.*, 1978) or a 'caretaker' (Archard, 1993b: 51–57) of the child's good. These descriptions are apt whether one believes the parent has rights over the child or merely has a duty of care to discharge.

But what is the content of the duty of care? In Chapter 1 I noted the difficulties of interpreting what is in a child's interests by reference to what the child would choose as an adult. I also noted not only that even a straightforward appeal to best interests could be open to contested interpretations, but also that there are problems in understanding what is meant by 'best' in 'best interests'. To re-emphasize the relevant point, we might distinguish between a maximalist and minimalist demand upon the parent in respect of a child. The former requires that a parent ensure that the child receives the best upbringing, the latter only that the child receives an upbringing that satisfies some basic threshold of acceptable care.

Note that the maximalist demand is ambiguous between two claims. The first is that particular parents shall do the best that they can for their children. The second is that particular parents shall give their child the best upbringing possible. The distinction here is between what is the best that some set of parents can do for a child and what is the best that could be done by *any* parent for that child. The 'best possible upbringing' might well be one that particular parents cannot themselves provide. It may be possible for *some other* parents to provide it, but not for them. Obviously there is a limit – in terms of a parent's circumstances and personal abilities – to what she can do for her child. Another possible guardian might be able to do more. Here, I shall reasonably interpret the maximalist demand to mean the first claim, not as requiring that parents be under an obligation that is impossible for them to satisfy save at the price of giving their children to other, better, parents. Indeed, were we to insist that each child is entitled to the best upbringing possible, some adults would simply not be permitted to have children.

Bigelow *et al.* draw a distinction similar to that between a maximalist and a minimalist demand on parents. Theirs is between 'perfectionist paternalism', whereby adults are obliged to do what is *best* for a child, and 'protectionist paternalism', whereby adults must only ensure that the child suffers no *harm* (Bigelow *et al.*, 1988: 185). Of course, non-malificence differs from beneficence. Ensuring that a child is not harmed is a weaker requirement than guaranteeing that the child is benefited up to some stipulated minimum level. On their account, the threshold of acceptable parental care is set very low.

It is implausible to think that parents *must* do the best by their children although, of course, they may strive to do so. But it cannot be specified as a duty, as to do so would be too demanding. The defensible requirement is that each parent should provide her child with the minimum standard of care. Furthermore, an adult should not procreate if she cannot reasonably guarantee that her child will at least have a life worth living. It is proper to talk here of reasonable probabilities since no parent could foresee an utterly unexpected disastrous course of events which left her bereft of the capacity to care for her offspring. What is the minimum standard of care? We might invoke the influential Rawlsian idea of primary goods, those goods that adults, as rational agents, would choose to have supplied to them as children (Gutman, 1989). We do need to emphasize the key value of autonomy. As we shall see in Chapter 3, there may be reasons for the state and society to ensure that its future citizens are equipped with the capacities to participate in the management and government of their community, and these capacities may amount to the possession of autonomy. But, arguably, adults themselves also have an interest in being autonomous, and, if this is so, they have an interest in a certain kind of autonomy. As we noted in Chapter 1, this need not be an interest in being maximally autonomous, in having as open a future as possible, but it is at least an interest in being minimally autonomous. Again, as we saw earlier, such an interest gives force to the argument from pluralism.

What duties do parents owe to other adults who may or may not themselves have their own children? As it seems clear that we should not strive to create additional human beings in a context of extremely scarce resources, the state has a legitimate interest in controlling population and may, as in China, enforce a policy of limiting the number of children a couple is allowed to have. Conversely, where numbers are dwindling the state may have an interest in encouraging adults to have children. We should not create a child whose existence in itself poses a threat to the lives and well-being of others as, for example, would be the case if the child were to carry a highly infectious and eventually fatal disease. In general terms an adult is obliged not to have a child if doing so within a specified context significantly worsens the life prospects of an already existing person.

Some might argue, further, that a parent is responsible and must thus compensate others for the harms her child does even as an adult (Vallentyne, 2002). This will strike most people as an unduly stringent requirement. A parent is surely not to be held responsible for the wrongs her child does as a responsible adult agent. A parent is arguably responsible for the harms her child does as a child, if the child's dispositions to cause harm can reasonably be imputed to failings in the parental upbringing. Nevertheless, it does not follow that a parent should suffer penalties for these harms. Vicarious punishment is viewed by most as unjust, even if some have seriously considered implementing it.

We can, of course, also ask whether those without children owe anything to parents. Having children affects other people, as we have seen. Third-party effects of an activity – that is, effects on those not engaged in the activity – are known as 'externalities'. These, in turn, may be either positive – that is, benefits or goods – or negative – that is, harms and costs. So, for instance, positively children supply society with future skills and productive capacities, whilst negatively they will consume scarce resources. We can also acknowledge that parenting children is costly. They need to be fed, clothed, watered, medically tended and educated. It follows that if one thinks that children produce only or, on balance, positive externalities, one could conclude that the costs of parenting should be shared between the custodial parents and the rest of society (George, 1987, 1994). Others think that even if parenting produces positive externalities, it should not be a subsidized activity (Casal and Williams, 1995).

This is neither an idle nor an abstract matter, since the costs of educating and providing health care for children may be borne by all who pay taxes, irrespective of their status as parents or childless adults. Although it is true that we all benefit from having received these subsidized benefits when we ourselves were children, nevertheless those who do not themselves have children must, if they pay the same taxes, pay a share of the parenting costs incurred by an activity in which they do not participate. This is not analogous to taking part in an insurance scheme to protect oneself against the costs of a possible outcome, such as subscribing to a national or private health system regardless of the frequency or severity of one's illnesses or even one's lack of illness. For many cannot have children, and others deliberately set their face against doing so.

Just Families

Raising the question of what might be owed to parents by society broaches the issue of justice, for we are asking whether justice requires that the costs of parenting should be shared by all including the childless. In fact, the relationship between the family and justice is a complex one and has many features. Let me separate these and discuss each in turn. Political philosophers in the English-speaking tradition have only recently turned their attention to the problems of the family. As Kymlicka observes, 'The family has not so much been relegated to the private sphere, as simply ignored entirely' (Kymlicka, 2002: 398). At the outset, then, it is proper to assess the claim that the family is 'beyond' justice – that it is simply inappropriate to think of the family as the subject of justice. There are two ways in which this claim could be pressed. The first is that the family belongs essentially to the private non-political domain and that it is only within the political domain that principles of justice apply. However, this is of course simply to beg the question. For it may be that the family does belong to the political domain and does so precisely because it ought to be governed by principles of justice.

The second way to press this claim is by appeal to the fact that the family is a sphere of affect or emotion; it is constituted in significant part by the relations of love and care that exist between its members. This, it might be said, makes it unsuited to the operation of principles of justice. We encountered this claim in Chapter 1 as part of an argument for the inappropriateness of according rights to children. Here we can add the following. Affect or love is itself something that is distributed, even if its distribution is not under our deliberate control. In previous times and in other societies love has been regulated; now the objects of our love are not chosen for us. But, however affect is distributed, it is distributed unequally to the extent that we love only some people, or at least love some more than others. The family may, as we shall see, be a source of economic inequality, but it is most certainly a source of affective inequality. The family is 'an emotional unit within which love is hoarded and passed on' (Walzer, 1983: 229).

It might also be considered a matter of justice whether or not an individual can found a family. There are at least two ways in which a person would be unable to exercise her right to found a family, even if such a right was protected by the state. The first is if the individual is infertile. The state could meet this problem either by subsidizing methods of assisted reproduction or by supporting a system of adoption. The latter might be in the interests of children who would otherwise lack custodial parents. The former, as we suggested earlier, needs further argument, but such an argument could appeal to considerations of justice.

The second way in which an individual would be unable to exercise a right to found a family is if she lacked the material means to guarantee that any child of hers would be able to enjoy a minimally decent life. As we saw earlier, the right to have and to rear children is constrained by the requirement to ensure that any child can reasonably be expected to have a life worth living. If an individual were unable to guarantee her child such an existence, this might well be a matter of justice. But it would be so only derivatively. For if an individual was incapable of caring for her own child, whilst others could, she would be suffering a level of material deprivation that might in itself merit the charge that her society was unjust. Justice might demand that she possess sufficient social and economic goods, and do so independently of the fact that she had need of such goods to provide for her children.

I say that justice *might* demand as much, because it could be that a just society is one in which the minimum that anybody should receive in terms of social and economic goods is also sufficient to allow a person to care for a child. But this need not be the case. The socially just minimum might not be enough to permit parenting. Further, there are a range of circumstances in which someone could reasonably be held responsible for reducing herself to a state below the minimum necessary to be a parent. With defensible principles of justice society can consistently assure everyone of a basic set of goods, yet not guarantee that everyone has enough to be a parent.

Turning to the relationship between the family and justice, the most important distinction to be made is that between intrafamilial and interfamilial justice. One question is whether the family should be regulated by the same principles of justice as rule society at large. A separate question is whether there should be justice between families. I shall take each in turn.

Should the family be just? We owe the most influential recent account of what justice requires and of what a just society looks like to John Rawls (1972). He believes that the principles of justice regulate what he terms the 'basic structure' of society. This consists of its major political, social and economic institutions such as its legal system, its constitution and its principal economic arrangements. Rawls includes the family within the 'basic structure' (Rawls, 1972: 7, 462–63) and, in his later work, *Political Liberalism*, he states that the 'nature of the family' belongs to the basic structure (Rawls, 1993: 258).

Clearly, some forms of social association – such as a church, football club or choral society – need not be governed by principles of justice. Indeed, for these essentially private associations of civil society rules of justice are simply irrelevant. Why, then, should the family be included in the basic structure? Rawls thinks that principles of justice should only apply to those institutions which determine – in a significant way and from the onset of an individual's life – how well someone fares and what social advantage they may reasonably expect. The family does, of course, play an important role in the determination of any person's life chances because it is a means by which the differential advantages or disadvantages that parents possess are passed on to their children. Indeed, it is because it does this that, as we will see, some, including Rawls, think that the very existence of the family is inconsistent with the realization of full social justice.

That, however, is the problem of justice between families. Here we are tackling the different question of why the internal structure of the family should be just. Here, Rawls may be misunderstood. In defining a basic structure he speaks about how the major institutions 'fit together into one unified system of social co-operation' over time (Rawls, 1993: 11) as well as the 'nature of the family' as within the basic structure. Arguably, then, he does not intend that principles of justice should apply directly to the internal structure and operation of each family. Rather, he means that the various possible forms of the family should be consistent with the role the family plays in reproducing a just society (Lloyd, 1994). However, even if that is how we should understand him, it could still be argued that the family can only play that role if it is internally just.

I will examine that putative role shortly but, first, we should be clear what it means to say that the family is just. On Rawls account, which most now follow, principles of justice regulate the distribution of primary social goods – that is, rights, liberties, powers and opportunities, income and wealth. Now we may distinguish between familial and general forms of these goods. Thus, as an example of the former, we have the rights and powers possessed by a parent, or the income which a parent or child possesses only in so far as she is a member of the family. As an example of the latter, there are the rights and liberties of a citizen, and the income that a member of society has command of. Is the family just if familial primary goods are distributed fairly? Clearly, unless one is a child liberationist, there is going to be an unequal distribution of liberties and powers. A parent has the freedom to make familial decisions that her child lacks. And what of familial wealth? This will probably not be distributed according to a principle of justice. Even if the children of a family each receive the same amount of pocket money, they will not be given that money with a view, say, to maximizing their position as the worst-off members of the family which is what Rawls's second principle of justice, the difference principle, requires.

However, one might insist that a family is just only if its *adult* members enjoy equal familial rights and a fair distribution of familial income. Indeed, feminist criticisms of the traditional family were directed at what was perceived as an unfair division of domestic roles which, they argued, resulted in the woman being engaged in a disproportionate amount of labour within the home without proper remuneration. It might be counterargued that, so long as the adult members of a family enjoy equal civic rights and liberties, any inequality of status within the family is irrelevant. Nothing, it could be said, of what goes on with the home should, or could, make a difference to the fair distribution of the primary *social* goods. Husband and wife are both guaranteed their equal rights under law and constitution.

However, things are not that simple. It may be argued that a gender-structured family helps sustain gender-structured social arrangements and, indeed, that familial injustice is the 'linchpin' of social injustice (Okin, 1989). First, if, as charged by feminists, women are largely confined to the fulfilment of their disproportionately burdensome domestic labours, then they are, to that extent, less able than men to act as citizens (James, 1992). The thought is this. The freedoms to vote, to stand for political office, publicly to speak one's mind, are negative liberty rights. But individuals may exercise these rights to varying degrees: they may take up a greater or lesser public role. To the degree that women are occupied within the family home playing the role of wives and mothers they are less able to play the public role. Feminist criticism of the public–private divide has classically focused on the disappearance of women from the public sphere and their absorption into the private domain of the household (Pateman, 1987).

Second, familial injustice may subvert public, social and political justice in respect of the role of the family in the moral education of the citizenry. If a just society is to reproduce itself over time it is important that, as they grow up, citizens acquire the capacities necessary for them to endorse and support the regulative principles of justice. As we have seen, children will almost certainly be brought up in families, and it is thus families that must play a major part in ensuring that a society's future citizens acquire the requisite capacities. Chief amongst these is what Rawls himself calls a 'sense of justice'.

Now, if the family is going to play this educative role, there arises an argument to the effect that children can only learn justice in just families. John Stuart Mill provides an admirably clear and direct statement of the view that families are 'schools of justice'. Mill was critical of existing nineteenth-century familial structures characterized by the subjection of women and prescribed the required alternative:

> The family is a school of despotism, in which the virtues of despotism, but also its vices, are largely nourished. Citizenship, in free societies, is partly a school in equality; but citizenship fills only a small place in modern life, and does not come near the daily habits or inmost sentiments. The family, justly constituted, would be the real school of the virtues of freedom. It is sure to be a sufficient one of everything else. It will always be a school of obedience for the children, of command for the parents. What is needed is, that it should be a school of sympathy in equality, of living together in love, without power on one side or obedience on the other. This it ought to be between the parents. It would then be an exercise of those virtues which each requires to fit them for all other association, and a model to the children of the feelings and conduct which their temporary training by means of obedience is designed to render habitual, and therefore natural to them. The moral training of mankind will never be adapted to the conditions of the life for which all other human progress is a preparation, until they practise in the family the same moral rule which is adapted to the normal constitution of human society. (Mill, 1984: 294–95)

The family can play an important educative role because, in addition to obedience, parents instil in their children certain moral dispositions as a matter of 'daily habit'. But it cannot morally educate future citizens to the acceptance of the principles that govern society unless it is itself governed by those self-same principles.

The 'school of justice' argument admits of various forms. In Mill's case it is a claim that parents teach their children values by example. One might also argue that children acquire, in their psychological development, the gender roles played by parents, so that girls grow up to be the kind of woman their mothers were. In this way, gender inequality is reproduced across generations. The 'school of justice' argument may also assume a more general form. Thus, if one thinks that a liberal society requires its citizens not only to have a sense of justice but also to be autonomous, then one could conclude that families must inculcate that capacity in its children. This would provide a reason for insisting upon the reform of certain kinds of family – those, for instance, that preach and practise religious fundamentalism (Exdell, 1994).

The key claim – that families 'school' future citizens in the values by which they live – is an empirical one (Okin, 1994: 38, fn. 32) and, as such, it is open to refutation. A common-sense rejoinder is that many feminists themselves were brought up in traditional families with a gender-based division of domestic labour (Lloyd, 1994: 364–65). Would it not in fact make sense to suggest that we learn the value of justice from unjust families, by identifying the relevant wrong, sympathizing with the position of the unjustly treated family member and protesting against a private injustice which the public rules of one's society ought to forbid? Indeed, one's sense of justice and commitment to its principles might be the stronger, the closer one's personal familiarity with injustice. One could also point out that the theory of psychological development that seeks to explain adult gender roles as a result of one's parenting is controversial (Cohen, J., 1992: 280–85).

Nevertheless, there is one final thought in favour of the view that families ought to be just, namely that there is something jarring in the idea that the structure of society should be governed by rules of justice, but that, at the same time, individuals within that society do not conform their own behaviour to these rules. Rawls himself thinks that principles of justice regulate the basic structure but not individual behaviour within it. However, that seems implausible, especially if one remembers that individuals must be motivated by a sense of justice that leads them to endorse and support these principles. Why, then, should not these same principles govern their whole lives even when part of these are conducted in private? (Cohen, G.A., 1997).

Having said that, there is, from the other side, one last

thought that speaks against regulating families by principles of justice. This is an argument from liberty of choice. An unequal division of domestic labour could be willingly and deliberately practised with either adult partner assuming the major domestic role and with a view to maximizing overall familial income. It is also the case that some women embrace a traditional understanding of their gender's role as domestic helpmate to the male. A key element of Rawlsian liberalism is that individuals should be as free as possible to pursue the good life as they understand and endorse it within the overall structure of a just society. Why, then, should not traditionalists be free to organize and live their family life as they see best (Russell, 1995)? Moreover, as we have seen, liberals are favourably disposed towards a pluralism of lifestyles. To insist that all families conform to a feminist template of familial justice would be to impose one doctrine of the good life on those who do not subscribe to it (Lloyd, 1994: 356–57). In sum, anyone insisting that families be just in the way feminism understands this requirement must show either that the choice of an unjust family form is not freely made or that such a form can, and does, subvert the justice of the basic structure.

What, then, of interfamilial justice? Rawls thinks that the existence of the family is an obstacle to the full realization of a liberal principle of fair opportunity and even asks, rhetorically it would seem, if the family ought to be abolished (Rawls, 1972: 74, 301, 511). What is the problem? The family is a means by which parental advantage and disadvantage is passed on to children. This is done in a number of ways. First, causal parents transmit genetic traits to their offspring. Second, families profoundly influence the development of a child's innate skills and capacities. They can do this not only in virtue of the material circumstances of the family but also in virtue of the parents' abilities to parent. Third, parents can, by gift and bequest, pass on material goods to their children.

Liberals subscribe to a principle of fair opportunity that insists that those with the same natural abilities and skills should have the same chances of success in life. Yet, if the family does serve to pass on differential advantage and disadvantage in the manner suggested, fairness of opportunity cannot be realized. To illustrate the point dramatically, identical twins should be equally likely to achieve success in their careers, but if they were brought up in different families – one better off in every sense than the other – then they will fare differently in their adult lives (Vallentyne and Lipson, 1989: 28).

The problem at issue has been characterized as a 'trilemma' for the liberal by Fishkin (1983). By a 'trilemma' Fishkin means that the liberal endorses three principles whose simultaneous satisfaction is impossible. The liberal must give up at least one of these principles to resolve the trilemma, but no one of the three, Fishkin thinks, offers itself as a candidate for rejection. The three principles are merit, equal life chances and family autonomy. The second has already been spelled out. The first is that positions should be fairly allocated on the basis of appropriate qualifications. The third is that consensual relations within any family relating to the upbringing of children should not be interfered with save to ensure a minimum standard of rearing – chiefly, that the children are able to grow up to take their part as adults in society.

Bluntly put, the liberal cannot have everything she wants. If she wants to retain the institution of the family she cannot realize equality of life chances so long as offices and jobs are allocated on merit. If she wants to ensure that all within society have equal life chances and award positions on qualification, then she cannot allow families to continue bringing up children as they see fit. The problems go right to the heart of core liberal egalitarian principles. That children are favoured on account of their familial provenance is deeply unfair in this regard. For the child it is a matter of brute good or bad luck which family they are born into and raised within. But, for the liberal egalitarian, inequalities in life prospects due to factors that are not the individual's responsibility are precisely those that ought to be removed or compensated for. On the other hand, the liberal wishes to leave the individual adult free to lead her life as she sees fit (so long as her choices are consistent with a similar liberty for others). Joining with another adult, forming a family, and bringing up one's children according to one's own outlook on life is surely one very important and highly valued manner in which this freedom is exercised. How, then, should the liberal respond?

One response is that the liberal ought not to be as strongly committed to the principle of family autonomy as to the other two principles (Vallentyne and Lipson, 1989: 39–40). After all, we have given reasons in this chapter to doubt the obviousness of the view that parents have a claim to bring up their own children when that claim does not derive from the prior interest of children in being brought up in the right way. Yet if in respect of the family it is the children and not their parents who are the prime subjects of any theory of justice or equal concern, then it is the principle of equal life chances that has real weight. A principle of family autonomy has no comparable weight or independent warrant. Moreover, we can surely think of family autonomy as being a matter of degree. We can envisage the construction of institutions, the implementation of laws and policies, and other measures that constrain the exercise of family autonomy – that is, the extent to which parents can simply pass on advantages (and disadvantages) to their children (Macleod, 2002). For instance, inheritance laws may circumscribe the extent of any bequest by parents to their children and educational policy may determine whether parents are able to exploit their social and economic advantage to secure a better school for their children.

Nevertheless, it will still be said that the family *in some form* remains an obstacle to the full realization of principles of justice. There are limits to the degree of official intervention in family life that are conscionable, and the only imaginable alternative to some degree of family autonomy is a Platonic system of official state nurseries and schools which would entirely replace the family and in which children would be brought up not by individual parents, but collectively. At this point, the liberal might simply insist that there is a necessary trade-off between the value of justice and those values of whose realization the family is a precondition. These latter values would be those, for instance, of affective closeness, intimacy and interpersonal commitment.

But the liberal might make a stronger response from the perspective of justice. For instance, if a just society is to be reproduced over time it needs the support of the citizenry and, as we have seen, that requires that individuals have a 'sense of justice'. However, there is no institution within civil society that can realistically be expected to play the role of moral educator other than the family. Families are the means whereby just citizens are made, and, arguably, are alone equipped to fulfil this function. Again, any alternative to the family – such as a state-managed nursery – would be much more destructive of individual freedom and autonomy, and it is these goods that a just society seeks to maximize and fairly distribute (Munoz-Dardé, 1998).

Finally, we might argue that principles of justice apply to human beings if they apply at all. But abolishing the family would mean that one could 'no longer be doing justice between full human beings, but between truncated people'. This is because being raised and living within families is an essential part of what it is to live a full human life (Taylor, 1985: 295). This is an interesting conclusion. An attractive and influential idea is that the good society can fully realize all of the ultimate values by which societies are appraised, such as justice, equality, freedom, decency and humanity, yet it may be that a completely just society cannot also be one whose members live fully as humans. Conversely, a society whose members live full human lives cannot also be perfectly just.

Summary

For all the criticism to which it has been subject the family, albeit in varying forms, has survived. Indeed, it seems an ineliminable element of our social life. In essence, a family is a stable association of adults and children whose main function is the upbringing of the children. It is in children's interests to be brought up within families, but it is less clear that adults have any right to found a family. If an adult does have a right to have a child of her own, it is constrained by the right of any child to have a life worth living and by the right of other adults not to have their lives significantly worsened.

We tend to assume that causal parents – those responsible for bringing a child into existence – have custodial rights to bring up any such child. Reasons for causal parents to be custodial parents can be derived from the interests of children. However, parents do not, as the proprietarian argument tries to show, own their children. Nor are children appropriately thought of as 'extensions' of their parents.

According to the 'priority' thesis, parental rights derive from a prior parental duty to care for the children. But it might be best to think instead of a parental discretion in the discharge of this duty. To discharge the duty parents must be paternalist. They need not do the 'best' for their children, although they must provide a minimum standard of care. Those without children may justifiably be required to assist with the costs of parenting.

Families are not somehow 'beyond' justice. Principles

of justice may not directly apply to each family as an institution, but just families may play their part in ensuring the reproduction of a just society. Justice between families may be necessary to realize important liberal principles. However, at the same time, full justice may only be achievable if the family is abolished, although doing that may sacrifice important values at the heart of what it is to live as a human.

Chapter 3

The State

So far we have considered the moral status of children. Do they, for instance, have rights, and, if so, which rights do they have? We have also looked at the putative rights and duties of parents. Do parents, for instance, have any rights over their children and what duties do they have in respect of them? The third party whose role needs to be considered if the picture is to be completed is the state or government.

I am going to argue in this chapter that the state has a role as *parens patriae* to protect the interests of children and a further distinct interest in ensuring that any current generation of children become society's future functioning adults. The state must thus ensure that children are educated to a certain minimum extent so that they can act as citizens. It must also, in its child protection practices, show a concern for the child's best interests but equally give due weight to the child's own views.

When balancing the state's role against the interests of parents I shall argue that parents do not, in virtue of being parents, have rights to determine what shall be done to their children. For their part, whilst children may be presumed incompetent to make decisions about what shall be done to them, this presumption is defeasible in particular cases. And children's views about what shall happen to them should always be given appropriate weight.

Clearly, the state and other public agencies have a role in enforcing the duties and in protecting the rights of children and parents. They do so most obviously if these rights and duties are legal ones. For instance, the 1989 English Children Act imposes on every local authority a general duty 'to safeguard and promote the welfare of children within their area who are in need' (Children Act, 1989, 17(1)(a)). The British government is also a signatory to United Nations Convention on the Rights of the Child. It thus has a duty to promote and to protect those rights that this Convention lists children as having.

But the state's role extends beyond the enforcement of legal duties and the protection of legal rights. In the first place, the state should provide public goods and promote the public interest. It may be naïve or simply false to think that the state always in fact does so. However, in ideal theory at least, it ought to and, crucially, it may be beyond the ability of individuals and private organizations to do so. Thus the creation of a transport and communications infrastructure, the protection of the environment, the maintenance of law and order, the provision of national defence and the promotion of public health all lie within the remit of the state. Further, laws and policies implemented in respect of these public ends will have implications for children and the family. For example, if law and order is at issue it matters at what age criminal responsibility is set and how the juvenile justice system is structured. In terms of public health there will be questions of what vaccination and inoculation policy is adopted, what forms of paediatric care are appropriate, and so on.

The foregoing might imply that the state has a role to play only in respect of those children within its own jurisdiction. However, this would be a mistake. The United Nations Convention on the Rights of the Child is an international charter, and those national governments that are its signatories have responsibilities towards *all* children of the world. States exist within an increasingly interdependent world bound together by multiple economic, political and cultural bonds. States cannot be indifferent to the global effects, both direct and indirect, of their own actions and of those of citizens, organizations and companies within their jurisdiction. To take a pressing contemporary example, the well-being of children is profoundly influenced by the level of a country's external debt. This is because moneys used to service loans cannot be used for health, education and other social services. Millions of children throughout the Third World lack access to basic education, die of malnutrition, suffer curable diseases and are compelled to work, often in dangerous and exploitative work (UNICEF, 2000). Western developed nations can be held accountable for the poor situation of children in developing countries. They are culpable inasmuch as their policies indirectly sustain this situation. If children do have basic human rights, all children, wherever they live, have them.

Within individual states children, I have argued, will be brought up in families. But I have not prescribed that all families in society should conform to any particular template. The idea that the state should assume sole and exclusive responsibility for the rearing and education of all young persons within its jurisdiction is beset by insuperable practical problems and is also subject to significant normative criticism. However, it does not follow from this that the state ought to play *no* role whatsoever in respect of children and families. I thus endorse two propositions. First, children should be reared in a family of some form. Note that, according to the minimal, stipulative definition of the family offered in Chapter 2, this means only that children will be brought up by some adult or adults with whom they have a continuing relationship. Second, the state should, nevertheless, play some role in the supervision and control of that upbringing. The scope and nature of that role is fixed by two very important considerations. These are the notion of the state as *parens patriae* and what I shall term the 'reproductive role' of the state.

The state is *parens patriae* – literally, the 'parent of his or her country'. In this role it provides protection to those who cannot care for themselves and who stand thus in need of protection. The classes of persons to whom the state acts as a parent includes, but is not exhausted by, that of children. It will also, for instance, encompass the class of the severely mentally disabled. Two features of *parens patriae* bear note. The first is that the state is only a parent 'in the last instance'. That is, the state only assumes parental responsibility in the absence of others and when there is a clear failure of parenthood. The 'state of families' – the model favoured in modern liberal democratic societies – is one in which children are, in the first instance, brought up within families. The adult members of families – those who assume the role of custodial parents – are also normally, as we have seen, the causal parents – those who have brought the child into being.

The state may assume the role of parent when there are no obvious adults identifiable as willing and able to assume the function of custodial parent. It may also assume the role of parent when those initially charged with caring for the child demonstrate themselves incapable of discharging their parental duties. This most obviously happens when a parent is found to have abused or neglected her child. The state as parent in the last instance does not literally and directly assume the responsibilities of bringing up a child, nor need such state provision mean that a child is reared in a public institution. A state may act as *parens patriae*, for instance, if it removes a child from its original custodial parent and reallocates it to an alternative custodial parent.

The second thing to note about *parens patriae* is that the parental powers of a state, once assumed, may be considerably greater than those possessed by adult citizens in their capacity as parents. The British courts have certainly thought so. In key cases that followed, and expanded upon, the *Gillick* decision discussed in

Chapter 1, the wide scope of *parens patriae* was affirmed. Thus it was stated that 'the inherent powers of the court under its *parens patriae* jurisdiction are theoretically limitless and that they certainly extend beyond the powers of a natural parent' (*Re W* [1992] 637). This means, for instance, that a court can ignore the refusal of a mature minor deemed 'Gillick competent' to medical treatment. This is noteworthy for at least two reasons. First, the import of the *Gillick* decision was – to quote Lord Scarman once again – that 'parental right yields to the child's right to make his own decisions when he reaches a sufficient understanding and intelligence to be capable of making up his own mind on the matter requiring decision' (*Gillick* [1986] 186). It would seem that the state's parental right of *parens patriae* does not similarly yield to the child's right. Second, the assumption by the state of the rights and powers of *parens patriae* is not undertaken in the name of the public interest. Rather, it would seem that the state is warranted in taking it upon itself to decide for the child because the child cannot decide for itself and the state must therefore do this for the child.

What is the reproductive role of the state? The state has an interest in securing the conditions of its own future existence. There is also, arguably, a broader public interest in social and political continuity that does not simply reduce to the demand that future generations should be fairly treated by the present citizenry. This reproductive role is displayed in a number of areas. Thus, for instance, a state has a legitimate concern with population levels. If a population grows too large it might threaten the viability of society by putting extreme pressure on available food resources. Equally, if the population declines beyond a certain point there may also be the dangerous prospect of a future workforce that is too small to fund the support necessary for what will be a disproportionately numerous group of old age pensioners. Again, the state should be concerned to secure the environmental resources – for instance, cultivatable land and energy sources – that are a precondition of a flourishing economy.

The relevance of children to the state's reproductive role is obvious. At its simplest, children are the society's future citizens, workers, army, lawyers and politicians. A state aiming to secure the conditions of its future existence, and that of the society over which it has jurisdiction, must be concerned with children and their upbringing. Indeed, it is often pointed out that the state's assumption of the role of *parens patriae* may in fact be motivated by a concern for this future. For example, the British state's first serious child protectionist laws and policies date from the beginning of the twentieth century. At that time there certainly was shock at the revealed condition of children unable to protect their own interests, the extent of child poverty, overcrowded housing, illiteracy, and poor general health. But there was also concern at the large number of young recruits to the army who failed their medical examinations, and at the threat posed to social order by the large number of homeless and 'street' children (Behlmer, 1982).

A state needs its future citizens to be physically healthy if they are to enter the workforce as capable, productive individuals, but it also needs its young to grow up to be *citizens* – that is, to be able to play their part in the democratic governance of their own society. Of course, the relevant competence can be specified in weaker or in stronger terms. Does a citizen need only the ability to cast her vote as an expression of a preference between distinguishable parties, candidates or policies? Or does being a citizen require more – namely, an ability to understand the salient issues, appreciate what is at stake and participate actively, through debate, discussion and negotiation, in the formation of law and policy? We shall see the relevance of these possibilities in due course.

What seems crucial – at least as far as modern Western liberal democratic societies are concerned – is that the state works with and through families to secure its desired ends: it does not set itself up in opposition to the family, competing with it to bring up children in the appropriate way. There is an important reason for this. A key idea within liberalism – introduced in Chapter 2 – has been the distinction, and the importance of that distinction, between a public and a private domain. In its simplest terms the private is the world of the personal and the public is the world of the political and legal. Law and politics should not intrude into the private, and a central element of the private has been the familial. The family is, in the title of Christopher Lasch's book, a 'Haven in a Heartless World' (Lasch, 1977), a sphere of affectively intimate and close relationships enjoyed away from the harsh public glare of our shared social and political world. The state, it is assumed, does not step over the threshold of our family home; it does not trespass upon our domestic space.

The distinction between public and private is a disputed one. Furthermore, the line that separates them is shifting and not always clearly defined. At one time, for instance, the world of work might have been thought of as private; consider the etymology of 'private property' and 'private enterprise'. Nowadays the world of work is seen as public. The most misleading temptation is to think of what is private and what is public as matters of fact, and thus to believe that the distinction between the two marks out a real empirical division carving our social world at its joints. We then apply an independent normative principle to the effect that what is private ought not to be subject to public scrutiny and regulation. This is mistaken. What is private is what ought not to be subject to public control. Doing Ø is private just if doing Ø ought not to be legally regulated.

Thus we cannot say that the family is, as a matter of fact, a private institution and therefore ought not to be subject to state supervision and control. Rather, we must show that the nature of familial life and activity is such that these are properly beyond the scope of legal and political governance. But why as a general rule should we think that? When a husband physically assaults his wife in the 'privacy' of their shared home he is as guilty of committing a crime as if he had attacked her in a 'public' space. The sexual abuse of a child by her father is no less of a crime for being perpetrated in the family home. We can, however, say the following. The normal everyday activities of a family may be presumed to be such that they do not warrant the attention of public officials. This presumption is defeasible. If it can be shown that what is going on in the family merits official interest, no appeal can be made to the essential privacy of family life to block that interest. What is going on merits official interest if the behaviour of family members crosses a specified threshold beyond which it is deemed unacceptable. For instance, and most centrally, the liberal state leaves parents free to raise their children as they see fit. It does not do so because it views parenting as an essentially private activity with which it has no legitimate concern. Rather, it presumes that a parent's normal quotidian actions in respect of her child are not such as to merit official interest. It trusts that parents will devote themselves to their child's interests and safeguard its welfare. However, if it can be shown that what a parent is doing to her child crosses the threshold, then the state is not debarred from interfering in the family's life by the consideration that it is thereby trespassing upon a private domain.

Three comments about this picture of the relationship between the liberal state and the family are in order. First, working on the defeasible presumption that what goes on in a family – and, in particular, how parents treat their children – is not a proper concern of the state is advantageous. Families work best if they are allowed, as a rule, to lead their lives freely and without official scrutiny. States operating with such a presumption are spared the costs of subjecting families and children to continual supervision. Second, the threshold whose passing triggers official intervention into family life can be set at different levels. Of course, a crime is a crime wherever it is committed. Assaults upon the person are criminal even if the other person is a family member. Nevertheless, I grant that what constitutes an assault may be thought contentious. Smacking a stranger in the street is a criminal assault. Smacking one's child in the home may be thought merely to be reasonable parental chastisement. However, expressing things this way reveals the oddity of believing that there is a relevant difference between the two actions. Not counting as an assault on a child what would count as an assault if done to an adult surely displays our inconsistency in prosecuting crimes against the person. It does not show that there is a relevant difference between an unacceptable assault and acceptable punishment.

Intervention into a family need not only mean the prosecution of a crime. The involvement of public agencies in a family's life may be initiated by non-criminal activity that is nevertheless thought sufficiently serious to defeat the presumption of familial privacy. Most Western jurisdictions work with something like the rule that where there is a real risk of significant harm befalling the child as a result of parental action or inaction, then (but only then) official intervention is justified.

Third, it would be a mistaken oversimplification to view 'official intervention' as only taking the form of the prosecution of criminal activity and the imposition of legal sanctions. A whole range of public agencies can be involved with a family – social workers, community workers, health workers and welfare officers. Indeed, some writers insist that the modern family is more thoroughly 'policed' by such quasi-official professionals than might be suggested if one's model of governance was the operation by government of legal–coercive measures (Donzelot, 1980; Lasch, 1977).

In summary, liberal states presume that families are best left free to conduct their affairs in private. This does not amount to seeing the familial as essentially private and thus as falling outside the scope of warranted official action. The state can, and does, interfere in the private life of families. Indeed, arguably, it insinuates itself into that life through the actions of various public agencies. Its interference is provoked by behaviour that crosses a specified threshold. This interference is justified by the state's requirement to protect such rights and to enforce such duties as are possessed by parents and children. Further, the state has a duty as *parens patriae* to safeguard the interests of children when they are unprotected. It, also and finally, must protect the general interest of all in the continued stable existence of society and state.

How, then, are we to balance the three sets of interests that have now been fully displayed? In any particular context we must weigh the following considerations one against another. On the side of the child there is her right, or maybe only her interest, that some state of affairs is brought about. At the least, we must consider any of her expressed views about what should happen, giving that view a weight proportionate to her maturity and ability to understand matters. On the side of the parents there are also interests in what shall happen. We have cast doubt on the idea that parents do have a right to determine matters in respect of their child. But they at least have some discretion in the discharge of their parental duties, and their wishes should not be entirely discounted. We should allow for the possibility that those who are a child's parents have different, and possibly conflicting, views as to what should happen. They also have interests simply as adults that are at least equal in weight to those of their children. Finally, from the side of the state, there are public interest considerations.

An influential view of rights holds that they function

as 'trumps' over public and general interest claims (Dworkin, 1977). Thus imagine that, on balance and without reference to any putative rights, the overall best policy is one that involves bringing about Ø. However, somebody has a right which would be violated if Ø were brought about. Then it follows, on this account, that the government may not bring about Ø. So, if children do have rights, then there are things that the government in its laws and policies may not do, even if doing these things would otherwise bring about the best state of affairs. This account expresses a view of rights as very powerful instruments of constraint upon government action. It is, of course, also another reminder of why it matters a great deal whether children and parents have rights.

If children only have interests, even with a right that due account be taken of their views as to the promotion of these interests, then these interests must be balanced against those of parents and those of society at large. There is no reason to think that the interests of children, just in virtue of the fact that they are children, possess a greater weight than those of their parents. We must thus assess the relative weight of different interests involved in particular contexts. In the remainder of this chapter I will consider three such contexts: education; child protection; and medical ethics.

Education

It is arguably in every child's interests that she be educated to a certain level, whatever she herself might wish for. Beyond that point, she may be entitled to be educated to whatever level she may wish for. The argument for compulsory education is a classic weak paternalist one. Weak paternalism substitutes the decision of the paternalist for that of the other if two conditions are satisfied. First, the other is incapable of deciding for herself by virtue of some defect of or hindrance to her decision-making. Second, serious harm will very probably befall the other, if the paternalist does not choose on her behalf. By contrast, strong paternalism substitutes the decision of the paternalist for that of the other just if the paternalist judges the other not to be choosing in her own best interests (Dworkin, 1971).

Compelling children to undergo an education can be justified on weak paternalist grounds in so far, first, as children are incapable of deciding for themselves and, second, failing to be educated would seriously harm their adult selves (Gutman, 1980; Hobson, 1983). I have already examined the arguments for judging that children are disqualified from deciding for themselves in virtue of their incapacity. Why would a failure to be educated damage the adults into whom children grow? It seems evident that, if adults are to flourish within their own society, they need to be equipped with certain skills and abilities. Clearly, the skills that are needed will be relative to the society in which they live. Literacy, for example, may be necessary only within a society that employs the written word to communicate and to inform.

We can, nevertheless, have a fairly good sense of what an adult in a modern Western society must have if she is to make her way with any hope for realizing her life-choices. This will extend beyond the command of a certain amount of general information and beyond the grasp of certain cognitive skills, such as literacy and numeracy. It will also require that she is independent and capable of making her own choices in life. It seems clear that only an education up to a certain level can equip a child to take her place as a minimally competent adult within society.

It is worth noting that a paternalist justification of the compulsory education of children does not imply that education only has a functional value. It is for children's own good that they are educated. However, that good need not consist solely in the fact that children are able, as adults, to take their place in society. What an education gives a child – knowledge, and capacities of critical appreciation – may be valuable in itself. It would thus be mistaken to justify reading good literature on the grounds that doing so was a preparation for active citizenship. Reading good literature is part of being well educated (Barry, 2001: 221–25).

When education is compulsory, the compulsion is exercised not simply against the child, but also against the child's parents. It is parents who must ensure that their child attends an appropriate school or, failing that, provide the child with an education at home equivalent to that which she would have received in school. But if parents have a duty to ensure that their children are educated, do they have discretion in how that duty is discharged? Moreover, parents are most likely to live their lives by values which they would wish to see their children also acquire and live by. At the very least, they share a family life with their children in conditions that make it likely the children will also come to share the parents' values. This was the import of 'the shared life claim' discussed in Chapter 2. Can parents be content with seeing their children acquire values at school that are at variance or in conflict with those practised at home? If parents, for instance, have a right to practise the religion of their choice and a right to pass that religion on to their children are they not entitled to demand that their children should at least be educated in a school that does not undermine their shared faith?

These questions, of course, assume even more significance when it is not simply a question of passing on religious beliefs, but also of sustaining and reproducing a cultural identity. For example, the parents may be members of well-defined cultures whose identity is constituted in significant, but not exclusive, part by a shared religion. There have been influential legal judgments that have broached these issues. In the United States the most celebrated have been *Wisconsin* v. *Yoder* [1972] and *Mozert* v. *Hawkins County Public School* [1987]. In the first case the old Amish Order sought to secure an exemption from the requirement that their children must attend public school to the statutorily required age. They did so because they wished to prepare their children for life within the Amish community and feared that continued education beyond a certain age would subvert the children's future attachment to the community. In the second case, a group of fundamentalist Christian parents sued the Tennessee school board to prevent their children from being exposed to reading material whose content they, as parents, believed violated their deeply held religious convictions. In both cases, parents objected to a public education because, in their eyes, it annulled or subverted their own parental efforts to pass on to their children those beliefs that were constitutive of their adult way of life.

What can the parents legitimately claim against the state in its provision of a public education to their children? Consider two different versions of the complaint that might be made. If the school explicitly and directly taught that the parents' values were mistaken, then it would seem that the parents would have grounds to complain. There is no reason to believe that schools are entitled to teach that the parents' way of life is erroneous. But a school has no ground, at least within a liberal polity, to teach that *any* way of life is mistaken. Schools, and their teachers, should respect and tolerate the different ways of life that are led by the families whose children they take in through their doors.

However, the complaint might only be that the child should not be taught generally to think about values in such a fashion that the child may come critically to reflect upon and, perhaps in consequence, reject the values of her own family. Such a complaint would not be warranted, for the complaint would merely be that the child should not acquire the capacity critically to think about and, if appropriate, to revise or repudiate the values she has inherited from her parents.

Parents may complain that the 'mere exposure' of their child to alternative views is discriminatory or violates their rights, for instance, to the free exercise of their religion. They may do so even when the school does not explicitly endorse these alternative views, nor openly criticizes their own views. Some writers support this complaint (Dent, 1988). However, it does seem possible to distinguish between the pejorative characterization of a group's way of life, or a parent's beliefs, and simply making children aware of the different ways of life and beliefs. Moreover, there is a clear point in making this distinction because children grow up within a broader cultural context that displays a diversity of lifestyles and beliefs and thus cannot avoid being exposed to the difference between their own familial values and others in their society. Being so exposed brings in its wake difficult and sometimes painful tensions, conflicts of loyalty and erosion of one's previously confident sense of identity. Yet such costs are the unavoidable price of cultural diversity and the tolerance of that diversity.

Parents cannot – as we saw in Chapter 2 – argue that they own their children, nor can they claim that children are, in some sense, merely an extension of their own selves. For neither of these reasons can parents claim that it is within their right to pass on to their children their own values without any interference from, or constraint by, the state. A possibility is an appeal to what I called, in the previous chapter, 'the shared life claim'. This, to repeat, does not show that parents have direct rights over their own children in respect of what the latter should think and feel, but does argue that, inasmuch as family members enjoy a shared life in conditions of affective closeness, children will tend to inherit the beliefs and values of their parents. Of course, these beliefs and values may be religious. However, the 'shared life claim' is an indirect argument for the plausibility of children acquiring the parental outlook on life; it does not ground a parental right to refuse an education in the understanding and tolerance of alternative outlooks.

From the child's perspective there is her putative right to an open future. I discussed this right in Chapter 1 and concluded that it should not be interpreted in maximizing terms as a right to the 'greatest possible extent' of future adult choice. It does, however, seem plausible to think that any such right should be interpreted in terms of sufficiency. A child should have *enough* adult autonomy to be able to make reasonable choices. If a child is brought up only to share her parents' values and beliefs, and is not taught of the possibility of alternative lifestyles or how to decide between them, then that right to an open future is denied her.

The child's right to be brought up to make, as an adult, her own life choices might also be defended by an appeal to public values which the children's own parents share – even when they appear or claim not to. I will consider two examples of such a defence. At the outset, let me offer a characterization of the imagined child's situation. Her parents hold fundamentalist religious views. They think that these views are not theirs freely to choose to hold or to reject. These views are derived from authoritative pronouncements of elders or from sacred texts, both of which lie beyond dispute. In some sense, then, the parents do not choose their religious views so much as see themselves as chosen as believers by the Truth. The parents do not, consequently, believe that their own children should, or need to, acquire a capacity of critical reflection and cognitive choice. Their children should simply acquire the truth.

A first reply by a liberal critic might proceed as follows (LaFollette, 1989). The parents assert a liberty right to live by their own values. But they cannot, consistently, assert such a right for themselves and deny it to their own children. If the parents expect their children to accept and live by their own parental values then they are denying their children the right they claim for themselves to choose their own values. However, this criticism will not work. The parents assert a right to the unobstructed practice of their values. They do not claim a right to the autonomous choice of these values. Indeed, they think of these values as *not* freely, that is autonomously, chosen. The parents esteem liberty not autonomy. They want their children to be able to live freely by values that they will not have freely chosen to accept or to reject.

Here is the second example of an appeal to public values to support a child's right to an open future. Arneson and Shapiro argue that 'in a democratic society that honors freedom of expression, state policy towards the education of children ought to be consistent with the underlying principles that support freedom of expression' (Arneson and Shapiro, 1996: 397). However, they add, this is true only if a right to free speech can be supported on the basis of a 'democratic faith' that the protection of such a right ensures citizens make more considered choices under the 'welter of considerations' generated by free speech (Arneson and Shapiro, 1996: 398). It would be 'quixotic' simply and bluntly to claim the right to free speech. Thus, if the parents value freedom of expression, then surely they must also value the ends that having a freedom of expression serve – namely the ability to make considered, informed choices.

However, this reply also fails. It is not unreasonable to assert other grounds for the right to freedom of speech than that it fosters autonomy. One might, for instance, cite the evils of censorship, the proper limits of legitimate government, the social utility of a diversity of opinions and so on. These are all plausible reasons for believing in free speech. In consequence, parents might consistently hold that their own views are not autonomously chosen *and* demand the right publicly and freely to proclaim them. It would not thus be incoherent for these parents to demand that their own children should proclaim, free of state law and policy, only those views that are acquired from their parents.

There is a possible indirect justification of the teaching of children to be autonomous that derives from what has been termed above the reproductive role of the state. In particular, the state arguably has an interest in ensuring that its children receive a civic education – that is, are educated to be citizens. A liberal state, if it is to reproduce itself, must guarantee that its future citizens have the minimal capacities necessary to function as participants in the democratic governance of their own society. The United States Supreme Court has recognized as much in a series of influential judgments. In the case of *Wisconsin* v. *Yoder* ([1972] 29) the Court concluded that the state had a legitimate interest in preparing 'citizens to participate effectively and intelligently in our open political system', to be 'self-reliant and self-sufficient participants in society'. In *Pierce* v. *Society of Sisters* ([1925] 1077) the Court spoke of the need to teach 'certain skills plainly essential to good citizenship'. Finally, in *Prince* v. *Commonwealth of Massachusetts* ([1944] 653) the Court talked of the dependence of a democratic society 'upon the healthy, well-rounded growth of young people into full maturity as citizens, with all that implies'.

What is required of a civic education and what is implied? A civic education must surely comprise an education in at least the following four elements (Citizenship Advisory Group, 1998: 6.8): concepts (such as 'democracy', 'law', 'citizenship' and so on), values (such as tolerance, equality and individual liberty), skills (such as an ability to understand and evaluate a political argument), and knowledge (such as how an election is conducted and of the basic constitution of one's society). These requirements can obviously be understood in fuller or in thinner terms, and, clearly also, how it is understood has implications for the content of any civic education. Amy Gutman, for instance, believes that a 'democratic society should educate all educable children to be capable of participating in collectively shaping their society' (Gutman, 1989: 77). John Rawls, for his part, thinks that, within a liberal state, the education of children should 'prepare them to be fully cooperating members of society and enable them to be self-supporting; it should also encourage the political virtues so that they want to honor the fair terms of social cooperation in their relations with the rest of society' (Rawls, 1993: 199). Indeed, there are a number of competing accounts of what exactly is required of a civic education within a liberal society (Macedo, 1995; Brighouse 1998; Galston, 1991).

The interesting question is whether the manner in which the requisite civic education is specified provides an indirect argument for educating children to be autonomous – that is, to have an open future. The argument is indirect in that it does not rest on the idea that it is in the *child's* interest to become autonomous. Rather, the state has an interest in its future citizens being possessed of the appropriate civic capacities. Even if they are not directly aimed at, these capacities may amount to the acquisition of personal autonomy. In this context, Rawls distinguishes 'political liberalism' from 'comprehensive liberalism' and the civic education that is associated with each. The 'comprehensive liberalism' of Kant and Mill would favour an education designed 'to foster the values of autonomy and individuality as ideals to govern much if not all of life' (Rawls, 1993: 199). By contrast, political liberalism does not endorse the ideal of the autonomous life and would not, in consequence, aim to educate children in such an ideal. It would require only the teaching of the constitutional essentials of society, foster basic political virtues, and instill the capacity to reason publicly as citizens.

Is a civic education in political liberalism the same in content and in its consequences as a civic education in comprehensive liberalism? Rawls seems to think so, stating that a politically liberal education would mean 'in effect, though not in intention' educating children in a comprehensive liberal education, that is to be personally autonomous (Rawls, 1993: 199–200). Amy Gutman has referred to this as the 'spill-over effect' whereby an education in personal autonomy is the by-product of an education in the skills of democratic citizenship (Gutman, 1985: 571). Other writers have also noted the coextensiveness of the two kinds of civic education (Coleman, 1998: 748).

Others have denied that the two kinds of civic education need be of the same kind. It might thus be argued (Wijze 1999) that a comprehensive liberal civic education privileges the disinterested search for the truth and the method of rational critical inquiry. It seeks to reinforce the comprehensively liberal ideal of the examined autonomous life. By contrast, the political liberal civic education is concerned only to provide future citizens with the knowledge of the various doctrines espoused within society. Whereas the former asks the child to examine and reflect upon the truth or falsity of any doctrine, the latter expects the child only to be able to recognize what the different views are. At the same time, the liberal civic skills of assessing political argument and debate do not amount to the skills of a fully autonomous person who can scrutinize her own life and choose how best to lead it.

These differences between a comprehensive liberal civic education and a political liberal one might be sufficient to persuade those parents who do not subscribe to comprehensive liberalism that their children need not be ideologically corrupted by the latter kind of civic education. Moreover, these parents might also be impressed by the following line of thought. Parents want their children to be free to live, as adults, the lives that the children value even if they may not want their children to be free, as autonomous individuals, to choose what lives they value. To the parents it can then be suggested that the freedoms of all citizens, whatever their ways of life, are only firmly guaranteed within a sustainable liberal order. Those parents who want to lead – and want their children to lead – non-liberal lives are best served by a liberal order that secures the freedom of all to lead whatever life it is that each person values. Such an order is, in turn, most effectively supported and sustained by citizens who have been taught the basic prerequisites of liberal citizenship (Macedo, 1995: 485–86).

Again, a liberal order is tolerant of diversity in lifestyles. Indeed, the argument from pluralism, considered in Chapter 2, examined the reasons why the liberal might highly value a pluralistic culture. Of course, these reasons had to do with the more fundamental liberal value of autonomy. Different cultures are valuable inasmuch as they are both the outcome of, and the invaluable background to, the exercise of autonomy. The parent who does not value autonomy – the fundamentalist believer, for instance – does not esteem diversity either in itself or as a precondition for other valued ends. The fundamentalist thinks that there is only one Truth to be believed and practised by all within society. Fundamentalist parents may also continue to insist that even a political liberal civic education is unacceptable. Inasmuch as it exposes their children to mere knowledge of alternative lifestyles and at the same time equips them with the basic skills of critical evaluation, it thereby runs the risk of diverting them from the path of 'true' belief.

The problems are well illustrated by the case of sex education.[1] The government can point to the general social utility of providing children with information about sex, chiefly the reduction of unwanted pregnancies at a young age and the lesser incidence among young people of sexually transmitted diseases. However, even among people who can agree that sex should be taught in schools, there is considerable disagreement about *what* exactly should be taught and *how* it should be taught, for the evident reason that people disagree fundamentally in their moral attitudes to sex and sexuality (McKay, 1997). Some, at least, of the divergent views also derive from strongly held religious beliefs (Reiss and Mabud, 1998).

These disagreements will extend to a characterization of why it is in the interests of children to be sexually educated. For some, it will be important that children are sufficiently well informed to make their own sexual choices, whatever these might be. For others, on the other hand, children need only to know what not to do sexually and to acquire an understanding of the virtues of sexual abstinence outside the appropriate contexts. How, then, are these forms of disagreement about the content, mode and purpose of sex education to be negotiated?

Teaching sex without any moral content will satisfy no one. Those who hold traditional or conservative views about sex will insist that at least some forms of sexual activity must be characterized as beyond the moral pale. Those with liberal or libertarian views will contend that young people need, at a minimum, to appreciate the import or significance of sex. Sex occurs within relationships and can have a consequential impact that is not captured merely by talking, in morally neutral terms, of its biological features. Nor is it satisfactory to demand of a sex education that it retreat to a statement of agreed moral basics. Even the supposedly most fundamental moral principles at play in sexual activity are subject to different, and disputed, interpretations. It has, for instance, been argued that we could appeal to an ideal of 'respect for persons', meaning 'a concern not to obstruct others in their purposes and a concern to do what one can to help them to flourish' (White, 1991: 406).

However, people will disagree as to what purposes are worthy of respect and in what respects a person may be said to flourish. Those who disagree about whether homosexuality is a legitimate lifestyle or a debased perversion will not agree about what, if anything, must be respected. Again, the injunction 'promote responsible sexual behaviour' is, as Mark Halstead observes, unhelpful 'if one person's understanding of responsibility involves wearing a condom and another's includes not being in the same room as a member of the opposite sex without a chaperone' (Halstead, 1997: 327).

Another way of negotiating moral disagreement about sex education would seek to provide children with comprehensive, but neutral, information about sex. Various forms of sexual activity can be described in a descriptively neutral manner while, at the same time, making young persons aware of the different moral judgements that can be made of one and the same activity. However, this will still not be acceptable to parents who hold that some sexual practices are so morally abhorrent that either they should not be mentioned or, if they must be described, demand an accompanying moral health warning.

These problems with sex education suggest that where there is serious, substantive background disagreement between parents, it may be hard for all to agree upon a common curriculum. Of course, the claims of parents to dictate what their children learn at school is not one that should be conceded simply and solely because it is their children who are being educated. Chapter 2 sought to discomfit those who assume that parents have a special title over their own children and consequent rights to determine what shall happen to them. Nevertheless, parents are also adult citizens, and a state that seeks to retain its legitimacy should not lightly ignore their views. This is especially true when the demands for a certain kind of education derive from a concern to protect or preserve the cultural identity shared by a set of parents.

Yet a liberal state may give priority to its reproductive role and educate its citizens in those virtues, skills and beliefs that guarantee the future survival, and flourishing, of the liberal polity. It may simply discount the criticism of the resultant education made by those non-liberal parents on behalf of their children. If the interests of the children themselves retain a weight in these arguments, it must still be determined what these are. Even if the child does have an interest in an 'open future', it should be noted that this is not inconsistent with the acquisition of a set of values from its parents, or even from being educated at a separate religious school. It is entirely consistent with liberal principles that an upbringing or education should transmit to a child a set of values so long as the child is able to reflect upon these values, electing, as appropriate, to revise, abandon or endorse them for herself. The liberal does not require that the person have no ends or goals, only that 'no end or goal is exempt from possible re-examination' (Kymlicka, 1989: 52).

Given all of this, it is not evident that religious schooling is, for instance, inimical to a child's open future. The danger is of representing – as Arneson and Shapiro do, albeit for argumentative simplicity – the underlying contrast between a 'religious traditionalist' and 'a secular worldly way of life' in an unduly pejorative fashion. The latter advocates 'withdrawal' from the world whereas the former prepares the child for different ways of life (Arneson and Shapiro, 1996: 401–402). Some forms of religious education may prepare a child only for withdrawal from all forms of worldly existence save the religiously approved one. Yet it is also true that many religious traditions encourage criticism, rational deliberation and independence of mind (Burtt, 1996: 416–17).

It is also true that an autonomous personality needs a steadfastness of character, strength of resolve and the commitment to act on one's choices. Such psychological dispositions may only be acquired within familial and educational contexts that teach a determinate set of values. The liberal upbringing is caricatured as one that is anxious not to transmit any values or way of life to the child lest that somehow pre-empt the child's own eventual choice. Yet it is also a caricature to characterize the non-liberal upbringing as one that denies the child any opportunity of challenging and questioning its family's, and its culture's, values.

Finally, we should acknowledge that membership of a culture, the possession of an identity, may also be of great value to a child as it grows up. Raz and Margalit eloquently describe the value of such membership as 'an anchor for their [members'] self-identification and the safety of effortless secure belonging' (Margalit and Raz, 1995: 86). Enjoyment of that good may require some sacrifice of autonomy, but such a loss need not be so significant as to deny the future adult what has been described as enough of an open future. Nor need it lead the child to 'withdraw' from the world. By contrast, a truly 'open future' might be guaranteed only at the cost of rootlessness, and a lack of any real or firm sense of who one really is.

Education serves a further important social end. In Chapter 2 it was pointed out that the exercise of family autonomy is in tension with the realization of an equality of life chances. The family is the principal means by which differential advantage and disadvantage is transmitted from adults to their children. Education is one of the principal means by which this reproduction of inequality can be constrained, even if it cannot entirely be eliminated in this manner. Clearly, it is not just a case – if one's aim is to equalize life chances – of denying richer families the liberty to pay for a more expensive education for their children. Nor is it even a case merely of ensuring that public spending on education is roughly equal across all children in a society.

Some think, further, that equalizing life opportunities

requires extra compensatory spending on the education of less well-off children by, for instance, giving schools in disadvantaged areas a larger budget. John Roemer thinks that to equalize the future earning capacity of black and white children in the United States would require spending about ten times as much on the education of the former, per capita, as on the education of the latter (Roemer, 1999: 69). Others are sceptical about the extent to which a publicly funded education can equalize life opportunities (Fishkin, 1983: 68–75).

Child Protection

As we have seen, the state is *parens patriae* and in that role it seeks to protect children from the harms that may befall them at the hands of adults – often, sadly, those of the children's own parents and guardians. Child protection (CP) practice consists of a set of laws and policies enforced and implemented by a wide variety of official and semi-official agencies. There are various possible normative models of CP practice (Harding, 1991). What follows discusses the balance of interests, and possibly rights, within a broadly liberal model of CP practice, that is operative in most Western liberal democratic jurisdictions.

The agencies responsible for the implementation of CP practice include social work, educational, police, legal and correctional, and medical bodies all acting, frequently in structured modes of interagency co-operation, to protect children. They will be guided by law and by key principles such as that discussed in Chapter 1, the paramountcy of the child's best interests. The harms children may suffer include abuse – sexual, physical and psychological – and neglect.

These agencies can act either *ex ante* or *ex post*. They act in advance of any proven harms where they believe they can detect a high risk of significant harm that is preventable or ameliorable by their intervention. They may act after instances of proven harm in order to pursue any indicated treatment of the cause of the harm, and, where appropriate, to make a disposal of the child. Thus, for instance, in an instance of proven abuse, the abuser of the child might be prosecuted and the child herself removed from the home of the abuser to an alternative guardian.

The warrant for the actions of these CP agencies lies, as has been said, in the state's role as *parens patriae*. It should not, however, be forgotten that the state's reproductive role gives it a public interest in the health of a society's children. There is some evidence to suggest the existence of a 'cycle of abuse'. Those children who have been abused display a higher probability than those who have not of themselves growing up into adults who, in turn, abuse. There is, of course, no guarantee that the abused child will later abuse as an adult, but there is at least some measure of correlation between being a victim and being a perpetrator. A state has an evident interest in checking that cycle. It hardly needs to be added that the abuse of a child is also a criminal act that the state should prosecute.

The child has a right not to be abused or harmed, or at least has a clear interest in avoiding such harm. Article 3.2 of the United Nations Convention on the Rights of the Child specifies that state parties shall 'undertake to ensure the child such protection and care as is necessary for his or her well-being'. Article 19.1 further requires that state parties 'shall take all appropriate legislative, administrative, social and educational measures to protect the child from all forms of physical or mental violence, injury or abuse, neglect or negligent treatment, maltreatment or exploitation, including sexual abuse' (United Nations, 1989).

Set against the interests of the child in not being harmed, and those of the state in seeing that its children are not harmed, is the interest of the parents in what we might call 'family integrity'. This phrase defines the ideal prescription that children are best reared within their own families that are not, as a rule, subject to official regulation, supervision or intervention. Indeed, we could specify as a leading idea of a liberal model of CP practice the thought that the state should respect family integrity. It can do this best by not interfering in the lives of families unless it has a case for doing so, and, even then, it should do in the final analysis and to the least extent possible (Goldstein, *et al.*, 1973, 1979; Wald, 1975). Thus the first two of the five principles that Waldfogel lists as constituting liberal CP practice are as follows. First, 'a family should be free of coercive government intervention unless that family has crossed the line into what we have defined as abuse and neglect'. Second, 'coercive government intervention into family life should be used as a last resort and should be minimized to the extent possible' (Waldfogel, 1998: 79–81).

The ideal of 'family integrity' in the context of liberal CP practices has, then, a number of constitutive elements. First, the family is left free, in the first instance, to conduct its lives as it sees fit. That, in effect, means that parents are given the discretion as to how to raise those children for whom they have been given responsibility. Second, actions (or inaction) by parents within the family that crosses a specified threshold of unacceptable behaviour triggers government intervention. That threshold may be set higher or lower, and it may countenance not just the proven incidence of harmful behaviours, but also the significant risk of future harm being occasioned. Third, government intervention is in the last instance. It takes place after the threshold has been passed and after all other feasible measures to protect the interests of the children have been taken. Fourth, the intervention is minimalist. It is the least necessary to secure the general ends of the CP practice.

Liberal CP practice is guided by two important

principles that have already been discussed in Chapter 1. The first is, as Article 3.1 of the United Nations Convention expresses it, that 'the best interests of the child has to be a primary consideration'. The second principle is, again following the United Nations Convention in Article 12.1, that the views of the child in matters affecting its interests shall be 'given due weight in accordance with the age and maturity of the child'. CP practice has, historically and in practice, been guided by a further precept that has not been given canonical and explicit formulation as a legal principle. It is that CP practitioners should, as far as possible, seek to work with, and not against, the family. More particularly, CP practice has been guided by the goal of what we could call 'family reconstruction'. The need for intervention reveals a failing of some particular family, but that failing does not commend the dissolution or replacement of the family as the primary place for the child's upbringing. Rather, it indicates the need for reparatory and restorative work that returns the family to a healthy and normal functioning. Thus much CP work, after the event, is rehabilitative.

The ideal of family integrity reveals a deep unwillingness on the part of the state to trespass upon the almost sacred space of the family home. By contrast, the workplace has been considered an entirely appropriate sphere of government action to protect the health and welfare of young employees. As a study of the origins of British CP practices expresses it, 'To patrol industry on behalf of the young was England's Christian duty. To patrol the home was a sacrilege' (Behlmer, 1982: 9). The ideal of family reconstruction reveals an implicit recognition by the state that, within the family home, parents possess, and retain, rights that cannot lightly be constrained. As a study of the early years of American child protection agencies expresses it, these agencies 'aimed as much to reinforce failing parental, paternal authority as to limit it' (Gordon, 2002: 50).

The ideal of family integrity is the subject of trenchant feminist criticism because it suggests that there is a natural familial form into which the state does, or does not, intervene. Feminists disagree. On their view, even a radically non-interventionist state is responsible – by its laws, policies, and its reproduction of certain background institutions and practices – for the perpetuation of a particular kind of family – one, for instance, in which the traditional oppressive roles of women are maintained (Olsen, 1985; Smart, 1982). It would be a mistake, then, to believe that the family is possessed of a fixed nature which the law must respect. Rather, the law plays its part in determining what kind of family exists and is respected within any particular society.

How does the law understand family integrity? It is notable that contemporary legal instruments and international conventions speak rather more than they used to of parental *responsibilities* as opposed to parental *rights*. Consider, then, Article 18.1 of the United Nations Convention on the Rights of the Child. This requires states to 'ensure recognition of the principle that both parents have common [and the primary] responsibilities for the upbringing and development of the child'. It continues by specifying these responsibilities as having 'the best interests of the child' as the parents' 'basic concern'. The article does not, significantly, speak of any rights possessed by the parents, and their responsibilities are clearly duties to promote the best interests of the child.

The European Convention on Human Rights does, as do other legal instruments, speak of an individual's 'right to respect for his private and family life, his home and his correspondence'. Such a right to individual privacy specifies a sphere of the individual's life that ought to be protected from unwarranted invasion not just by the state, but also by all agencies, organizations and other individuals. We should be careful to distinguish familial privacy from parental autonomy. Furthermore, the putatively single ideal of family integrity is, in fact, constituted by both elements (Archard, 1993b: ch. 10). By familial privacy is meant the protected absence of official supervision of family life. By supervision we mean observation and regulation. The state, and its agencies, respects familial privacy in that it does not continuously inspect what a family does at home, and it does not require that these activities conform to a set of enforced rules of standard, or 'normal', family behaviour. To repeat, according to the liberal model of CP practices, the state only intervenes in the last instance.

By parental autonomy is meant the freedom of parents to rear their children as they see fit. As we saw in Chapter 2, this need not amount to a parental right to rear. It is only, at most, a discretion that parents may exercise in the discharge of a morally prior duty they are under to promote their child's interests. The talk in international conventions and legal statutes of parental responsibilities, rather than parental rights, would suggest that this is how the parental 'freedom' is now to be interpreted.

It is, of course, natural to think that parental autonomy and family privacy go hand-in-hand. They seem, conjointly, to amount to the idea that families should be left to their own devices. But they are separate, and separable, ideas. Nor need they be conjoined or entailed by one another. Parents could, conceivably, exercise discretion in their parental activities whilst being observed by officials doing so. Parents could also enjoy privacy in their family lives but be denied any discretion in their discharge of their parental duties. Of course, the immediate thought is that the strict regulation of parenting requires observation. The converse thought is also persuasive. If parents enjoy privacy and are not observed, then their parenting cannot be regulated. But – subject to an apparent paradox that will be explored in due course – we can insist that, although family life does, and should, enjoy privacy, parents do not, and should not, enjoy a liberty to bring up children just as they see fit.

What is the warrant for family integrity as defined? Parental autonomy reduces to discretion in the discharge of the parental duties of care for children already discussed in Chapter 2. What, then, is the value of familial privacy? The answer seems to be that both parents and children have an interest in sharing a life together under conditions of intimacy and affective openness. Arguably, this interest can only be secured and promoted if the family enjoys a measure of privacy. Being free of observation by other persons, members of the family can live together whilst openly expressing their feelings for one another. They can share activities, tasks and their leisure time without being under general scrutiny. Of course, families do not enjoy all of their lives removed from the public gaze: they may share space with others in many of their characteristic activities, for instance on holidays, at play or during schooldays. However, at least some of the time that a family spends together is valuable on account of being private. Indeed, the enjoyment of such shared time is what allows a family to be just that.

In short, a precondition for the possibility of the family being a valuable social institution is that it should enjoy a protected privacy. Moreover, the family is a valuable social institution not simply because it serves the interests of its adult and child members. Despite the criticisms of the family rehearsed in Chapter 2, it was acknowledged that the existence of families promotes valued social ends, such as the reproduction of diverse ways of life. This was the import of the 'argument from pluralism'. More generally, the family has long been viewed as a bulwark institution, standing between the bare, isolated, individual and a state that might seek to regulate all aspects of her life. As defenders of the family against its critics have often repeated, it has been the totalitarians – those desiring that the state should exercise total control over its subjects – who have tried, without success, to abolish the family.

By contrast, the liberal state, for its part, is content to leave the rearing of children to families rather than assume the task of directly caring for all of society's young. Yet, to repeat, coercive state intervention into the lives of families is triggered once a specified threshold of behaviour is passed. The operation of such a threshold is a function of at least two considerations. One is the level at which the threshold is set. The second is the extent to which behaviour crossing that threshold is detected. An analogy is provided by the operation of drink driving laws. This is also a function of, first, the specified legal threshold of blood alcohol beyond which a driver is criminally liable if in charge of his car and, second, the official manner in which such levels are detected. The operation of the drink driving law is only as effective as the means of detecting the violations of that law. It is for this reason that the introduction of the breathalyser – a more efficient and reliable detector of blood alcohol levels than previous methods – acted as a deterrent to drunken driving and did so independently of any change in the law or in its attached penalties.

Similarly, the operation of any CP laws and policies will only be as effective as the means that exist for detecting or predicting breaches of the threshold of child abuse and neglect. In most liberal jurisdictions the threshold itself is set – as it is by the English Children Act – in terms of 'significant harm'. This, in turn, will be defined, as it has been in the English context, as harm that is 'considerable, noteworthy or important'. The specification of the *risk* of significant harm that triggers intervention will also most likely be in terms of how serious it is. Moreover, in implementing any set of CP policies, practitioners will be guided by a body of past case practice. As in the operation of the law at large, general terms are rendered more precise and substantive through precedent and ongoing decision-making.

Yet in the matter of detecting, rather than simply defining, child abuse and neglect is there not an evident paradox? Evidence of harm (or of its serious risk) will warrant a breach of familial privacy. However, such evidence can only have been secured by having already breached that privacy. We can only know if parents are abusing their children, or risk doing so, if we, as officials, are able to observe their parenting. But does not the family's claim to privacy deny us the means of knowing when we are justified in overruling that claim? How do we know, if there is familial privacy, when there is harm to a child and a reason not to respect a family's privacy?

The solution to this apparent paradox is as follows. There are ways of detecting child abuse and neglect (or their serious risk) that do not breach familial privacy. One possible means is by the *ex ante* identification of a parent as high risk – that is, as someone exhibiting the profile of a child abuser. Some have attempted to devise a checklist of features that such a person would normally be expected to display (Greenland, 1987), but the use of any such profile is only as helpful as the profile is accurate. In addition, there will always be serious concerns about the implications of using a profiling technique of this kind. A dangerous person is somebody who might very probably cause harm. He is not somebody who has actually caused harm, and it may be inappropriate to disadvantage or burden a person who has not, as yet, done any wrong.

There are, however, other ways to detect child abuse or its serious possibility. A number of agencies regularly come into contact with children, and have the opportunity of assessing their general health and welfare. Schools are an obvious example. Children also pay visits to doctors who are trained to be alert to the possibility that the injuries or illnesses they detect are occasioned by the abusive acts of adults. Social workers are also often contacted by neighbours who are anxious to report any harm that they suspect may be being done to a child next door.

Nevertheless, there is no room for complacency. In so far as the liberal model of CP practice continues to respect familial privacy, much child abuse and neglect goes undetected. Even where a suspicion of such harms has arisen, a concern for this privacy may constrain an investigation that would otherwise uncover clear evidence of abuse or neglect. There is also evidence that social workers and other professionals charged with the care of children are unduly disposed to trust the good intentions of parents and not to suspect them of being abusers of their own children (Dingwall *et al.*, 1983). There is a further point. *Ex post* intervention – triggered by the discovery of serious neglect or injury – can be very drastic. For instance, such intervention may well take the form of the removal of the child. However, such action is also potentially damaging to the child; she may be protected from further abuse and neglect only at a considerable psychological or emotional cost. On the other hand, the harmful behaviour that has been disclosed, and which triggered the intervention, might have been prevented had work been done earlier with the family or if services had been provided to the family. That is, a lower level of familial intervention might forestall the need for a later and more serious breach of privacy, and, moreover, be in the better interests of the child (Bourne and Newberger, 1977).

CP practice is not exhausted by the identification of a problem of child abuse and neglect (or its serious possibility). Whether there is a single problem of child abuse is itself problematic – in other words, the question of whether there is a single enduring category of harmful actions and omissions in respect of children that can usefully be resumed under the title 'child abuse' is a very difficult one (Archard, 1998; Abrams, 1979). However, leaving that issue to one side, CP practice can be seen as being constituted by three moments. First, there is the identification of a (possible) problem. Second, acting on the basis of what has been identified as a problem, there is an investigation and an evaluation of the scale of the problem. Third, and finally, there is action. Such action will, in line with CP practice, be motivated by a concern to promote the child's interests and by a regard for the child's own views weighted according to the child's maturity and understanding of the issues. Clearly, such action can be of various kinds, ranging from voluntary work with a family through to the permanent removal of the child from the family and her reallocation to alternative guardians. To repeat, the imperative to work with the existing family and to rehabilitate the child is paramount among most CP practitioners.

In the action that official agencies might take in respect of the child there must be the same balancing of the respective interests as is conducted in the general specification of CP principles – that is, there are the child's interests, the parents' interests and the state's interests. The first and last sets of interests have already been adequately discussed, although it is interesting to consider what role parents can claim to play in any CP action. Clearly, where voluntary cooperation with the family is envisaged, and is feasible, the parents have determined that they will play a particular role – acting upon social work advice and, at the same time, having their own views given a weight by social workers. This is a case in which all parties are committed to resolving the particular intrafamilial problem that provoked social work intervention. Even compulsory, and legally sanctioned, social work involvement with a family may aim at repairing the family and, in consequence, give serious consideration to parental views. All of this is nevertheless consistent with a concern by the official agencies only to promote the interests of the relevant child. It may be that the child's interests are best served by remaining with its parents, but it is the interests of the child, and not any parental rights in respect of that child, that provide the ground for, and ultimately constrain, the terms of any social work action.

In those cases in which the family has broken down, or when the parents have revealed themselves to be irremediably incapable of protecting the child's interests, it is not clear what weight, if any, should be given to the parents' views in respect of the disposal of the child. When a child is reallocated from its original parents to alternative guardians it may be important for the child – in terms of her own sense of her identity and origins – that some form of contact is maintained with the birth parents. On the other hand, even the most minimal form of contact may prove disruptive to the new placement and disturbing to the child. Whatever is in fact the case, it is, once again, the child's own interests, and her views in respect of these, that matter. Parents do not retain a right to determine what shall happen to their own children simply and solely in virtue of being their parents. To think as much is to accord a brute, and ultimately inexplicable, significance to the biological relationship (Archard, 1995).

Before closing this discussion of child protection practices it is worth making one brief observation. The vast majority of liberal jurisdictions effect a clear distinction between the protection of children who have suffered harms and the treatment of those children who have themselves committed offences. Whereas social work, educational and psychotherapeutic agencies are deemed the appropriate ones to deal with the first class of children, the second are normally allocated to a juvenile justice system for some form of punitive treatment. There is an exception to this categorization provided by the Children's Hearings System that uniquely operates in Scotland and also provides an interesting case study for all other jurisdictions (Lockyer and Stone, 1998). Underpinning this system is the idea formulated by Lord Kilbrandon, the author of the report that led to the system's creation (Kilbrandon, 1995).

This is that children who are the victims of offences (such as acts of parental cruelty and neglect) and those who commit offences (of varying degrees of seriousness) are both equally children with problems. The way to address these problems need not be by means of disposal within a justice system but may instead be through the cooperative actions of CP agencies. It is not just that children may be inappropriately classified as criminal agents; it is also that the deep-lying explanation of their 'criminality' may be the existence of a problem that, in the absence of any offence, would best be addressed through social work and other agencies.

Medical Ethics

A child is normally presumed to be incapable of making her own decision in matters affecting her interests. Her views on these interests may be taken into account and accorded a weight proportionate to her maturity and understanding of the issues, but her own wishes as to what shall be done to her is not, as it would standardly be in the case of an adult, decisive. When decisions are taken in respect of a child they can be motivated by a concern for the good of the child or for the good of others. The disjunction here is inclusive – that is, a particular decision may be for the good both of the child and of others. Let me explore each possibility with respect to medical decisions.

Paternalism is making a decision on behalf of the other person in the light of that person's good. Paternalism or, more correctly, weak paternalism is considered to be justified when the other suffers from a defect or encumbrance of her decision-making capacities and when there is a probability of harm if the paternalist does not intervene. In short, the other cannot decide what is good for her and will choose badly if allowed to do so. We might add proportionality as a third condition. That is, the harm done by paternalistically intervening is warranted by the harm that is prevented, or good that is promoted, by intervening (Childress, 1982: 109). Indeed, some think that even weak paternalist intervention is justified only when it is intended to prevent a very great harm or to secure a very great good.

In Chapter 1, I introduced the idea of a 'mature minor'. This is someone below the designated age of legal maturity, and thus presumed incapable of making her own decisions, but who nevertheless displays a competence in respect of some particular matter. Such a young person may be designated 'Gillick competent' and thereby be deemed to have the right to make her own decision in respect of that matter. In Chapter 1, I also outlined what might be meant by Gillick competence and criticized the rather strict and demanding understanding of competence it stipulated.

In general, a principle of informed consent governs decision-making by mature adults in respect of their own medical treatment. This principle requires that a person is able to make decisions, does so voluntarily, and understands the import of any decision they might make. 'For a patient to be capable of giving informed consent she must be competent, must understand the information disclosed to her, and must give (or withhold) her consent freely' (Young, 1998: 442). It is important to emphasize the following point. The content of any decision made by a person is at most indicative of, but is not constitutive of, her incompetence, or indeed her competence. A decision may be bad in the sense that *what* is decided is inappropriate or mistaken or stupid. Recognition of this fact may lead us to doubt that the person making the decision is competent to do so. But the judgement that someone is incompetent to decide is strictly independent of the content of her decision. The latter may provoke an inquiry into her competence, but it is not a criterion, as such, of her incompetence.

What, then, are the elements of unimpaired nondefective decision-making? First, the individual concerned must understand what is involved in the making of the decision – that is, she must have a command of the relevant information and also an appreciation of its significance. She must, for instance, know the risked outcomes of a course of medical treatment and, alternatively, of not undertaking the treatment. Further, she must grasp what these outcomes will mean for her. Second, she must be possessed of a deliberative or ratiocinative ability – that is, she must be able to recognize the relationships between pieces of information and true general propositions, and, where appropriate, make correct inferential judgements. She must, for instance, be able to recognize that the risks run in undergoing an operation are risks from which she is not exempt. Third, she must have comparatively stable, enduring and consistent preferences – that is, she must want roughly the same things over time and not be too inconstant in her desires. Finally, she must be autonomous and independent – that is, she must be able to make up her own mind and be committed to executing those choices she has made for herself. She must, for instance, have a clear view of whether or not she wants the operation that she can communicate to the doctors.

These are general capacities. But we should acknowledge that some decisions are more momentous than others. These are ones that are more significant in their consequences – involving, perhaps, substantial changes to a person's life prospects – and they may be irreversible. It seems plausible to judge that the competence to make a decision is, to some degree, relative to the seriousness of the decision that has to be taken. For instance, someone contemplating whether or not to give blood does not need to be as cognitively well placed as someone deciding whether she should have a potentially life-saving operation that, nevertheless, carries with it serious risks of irreversible brain damage.

It nevertheless seems true that adults, in general, have the capacities to make medical decisions in respect of themselves that children in general lack. Yet it is also true that some decisions are surely beyond the decision-making capacities even of some adults. Can every mature person fully grasp the significance of certain important medical procedures? It is important to ask this question. The general background presumption is of adult competence and childhood incompetence. That presumption is defeasible in the case of children if they can be shown to be Gillick competent. It is not, by contrast, defeasible in the case of adults by showing some of them to be Gillick *in*competent. Put another way, the onus placed on children is to demonstrate that they are not incompetent. But adults are under no such requirement, even though it may be true of some children that they are as, if not more, competent to make certain kinds of decision than some adults.

The principle of informed consent also needs to be set in context. It would thus be a mistake to think in terms of a bare decision-making capacity exercised in respect of particular matters. The fact is that the context in which decisions are taken makes a difference. Evidence suggests that circumstantial factors may significantly affect the likelihood of consent being given by an individual to some course of action such as a medical procedure or to participation in medical research (Sugarman *et al.*, 1999). For instance, it makes a difference how information is given to the individual. This can vary in respect of its mode of transmission (orally, written, videotape), its level of difficulty and the amount of information transmitted. The circumstances in which information is imparted also makes a difference. Is it given by an authoritative figure, such as a senior surgeon? Are other family members present and exercising an influence on the decision-maker? In what mood is the decision-maker – under stress and anxious, hopeful or depressed? How the consent is obtained will make a difference – whether, for instance, it is secured orally, or by a written form, or simply by default in the absence of dissent from a proposal.

It should be clear that certain contexts are going to be more congenial to children understanding what is involved in a medical decision and also to ensuring that any views they express are their own. Thus circumstantial factors surrounding any medical decision should be sensitive to the child's needs and be arranged accordingly. Nevertheless, it remains the case that, in the taking of medical decisions, there is a general tendency to exclude any consideration of children's interests and views. This is counterproductive and unwarranted for at least four interrelated reasons.

First, the evidence suggests that involving children in their medical treatment makes them better patients: 'Research has shown that when children acquire knowledge about their condition, treatment, likely pain and prognosis, they are more willing to cooperate with treatment, they understand better when and why to take drugs, they endure painful treatments more patiently and recover better' (Mahall, 1995: 24). In general, the more willing and informed the patients' commitment to the treatment, the less the distress it will occasion. This is as true of children as it is of adults (Alderson, 1993: Ch. 11). Second, children who do not display Gillick competence should not be thought of as somehow lacking *any* understanding of a medical procedure. They might not be sufficiently mature to be presumed able to give their informed consent, but they might very well be capable of having some understanding – indeed, perhaps even a relatively clear and accurate sense – of what is happening to them.

Third, children are likely to have strong views about what shall happen to them, especially when a medical procedure may be painful or distressing. There is a duty to give the views of children a weight proportionate to their understanding of the issues. The more children know about what is happening to them, the greater their understanding of a proposed course of medical action and the greater the significance of their views. Medical professionals are thus duty-bound to try to explain to children, as far as they as they are able, what it is proposed to do to them and what it means. Fourth, medical personnel should be thought of as under a general obligation to explain to a patient what they propose doing to her. This is an obligation that is not the same as, nor follows from, an obligation to secure the patient's consent to the procedure. Even if a doctor does not need the patient to agree to his actions – because the patient is incapable of giving her consent – he should nevertheless tell the patient what he is going to do. A pediatrician observes good medical practice if he explains to a 7-year-old child what a lumbar puncture is. This is true whether or not he needs a 7-year-old's assent to the procedure (Mahowald, 1996: 96).

Should only the child and the medical practitioners, and no others, be involved in the making of any medical decision concerning the child? If the child is incompetent to consent to a proposed course of medical action, should the decision be left to the medical professionals? What of the interests of the child's parents? In some cultures, especially Asian societies deeply influenced by neo-Confucian ideals, it will be thought proper that the whole family makes a decision about what medically should happen to any of its members. Within the West, and under the influence of liberal individualist ideas, the interests of the child are thought of as distinct. A child is not simply a family member, but is also a separate individual. She may not, as yet, have the capacity to make her own decisions, but that does not mean that she is not possessed of her own interests and needs.

If the parents are to be involved in the making of a medical decision in respect of their child, it is important to be clear about the warrant for their role. As Chapter 2 argued, they do not have a role as the persons who purportedly own the child or as the persons of whom the child is a supposed extension. Yet, they may have a role to play as the individuals who are best placed to know what is in a child's interests, or they may at least be best placed to advise what it is the child wants when the child herself is incapable of expressing her own views on the matter. In discharging that role the parents are, of course, duty-bound to act for the child's, and not for their own, interests. From the side of the child it may be that her closeness to her parents vitiates her competence to choose for herself. A child may be capable of making a medical decision in the following respects: she understands what is involved; she possesses the ability to reason; she has comparatively stable, enduring and consistent preferences. Yet she may not be completely able to make up her own mind, for she may be unduly influenced by her parents and what they wish for her.

Consider a 10-year-old brought up within a Jehovah's Witness household and, in consequence, sharing her parents' religious outlook. She is in need of a kidney transplant and refuses an operation that cannot be guaranteed to be bloodless. She grasps the point of the medical procedure and the consequences of refusing it. Yet she could be judged not to be making her decision autonomously. She *may* subscribe to the religion of her family in an independent fashion, but there are reasons to doubt that she does. It is worth repeating that it is important not to let the perceived imprudence of her decision – refusing the operation, for instance – be taken as a criterion of her incompetence to decide for herself. The child's ability should be determined independently of the content of the choice she makes. If she is deemed to be competent to decide, then her choice – whatever it is – should be respected.

Where a child is undoubtedly incompetent to make a medical decision, parents and health workers may hold conflicting opinions as to what is appropriate. On the parents' part these conflicts may, or may not, derive from sincerely held religious beliefs. Medical staff may want health care for the child that her parents believe to be unnecessarily costly, painful or distressing. By contrast, the parents may want medical treatment for their child that the doctors view as beside the point (Elliott, 1998: 453). In line with what has been argued throughout this book, these parental views do not carry weight in consequence of any putative right, or claim, parents have to determine what happens to their own children. Parents remain bound by a duty of care for their children and are obliged to promote their interests. If what parents wish for their children is what they believe to be in the children's interests, then their views have weight. However, these views have such a weight not because they are those of the parents, but because they are formed by a concern for the child (Elliott, 1998: 454). Furthermore they have weight to the extent that parents are reasonably judged to be well placed to advise what is best for their child.

I said at the outset of this section that medical decisions taken in respect of a child could be motivated by a concern for the good of the child or for the good of others. Having considered the first disjunct, let me turn to the second. For some people, the following is evidently true. Parents could rightly insist that one of their children should undergo a non-therapeutic medical procedure – so long as it carried only minimal risks – if it was necessary to save the life of a sibling (Nelson and Nelson, 1995: 102). There are two ways of understanding this claim. The first is that the child is to be thought of as a member of her family with particular obligations to other members. On this account, she has a special duty to help save the life of her sibling, although she would have no such duty in respect of a stranger who was in the same life-threatening situation as her sibling. On the second account, the child *is* under a general duty of beneficence to promote the good of all, and it would be appropriate, given this duty, for her parents to make her available for those medical procedures that effectively discharged this duty. She might be better placed medically to help a sibling simply on account of such factors as the compatibility of tissues and organs. Note that, on either account, it is the parents who act to ensure that the child fulfils her duties, because we assume that the child is incapable of making her own decisions as to what it is best to do.

Let me take the first account first. Speaking of the child as being under a duty seems to be necessary if we are to avoid thinking that the parents are permitted to treat the child merely as a means to the end of saving a life. Compare the case in which the parents agree that the family pet can be used for some good veterinary or medical research purpose and in a way that does not involve any significant risk to the pet's life or any more than negligible discomfort. Here we do not think that the pet is under any moral obligation to help others. We do think that the family, subject to the constraints of the pet not being exposed to suffering or to the serious risk of losing its life, may dispose of the pet as it sees appropriate. In the case of the child, the duty to save her sibling falls upon the child herself. But why would we think that the child is under such an obligation?

Imagine that there was only the one sick child and, further, that one of the parents had the compatible tissue necessary to save that child's life. Would this parent be under an obligation to donate the tissue? To many, it would seem clear that she was. Others, however, might doubt that she was, and would believe that this would still be the case even if the operation the parent would need to undergo was comparatively risk-free and painless. Of course, most, if not all, parents would undergo the procedure in order to save their child's life, and they would do so from unconditional love for their child. But, in moral terms, their action might be more properly described as supererogatory and not as obligatory.

There may be special duties incumbent upon family

members and which are, to some degree, constitutive of what it is to be a family. These duties would be ones of special care. Thus, I may well think that I owe more by way of concern to my parents and to my siblings than I do to strangers and there are things I will do that display this special concern. But it is not clear that undergoing a medical procedure on behalf of another family member is something I am *required* to do just in virtue of belonging to a family.

On the second account, the child is under a general duty to help strangers. She can best discharge this imperfect duty by undergoing a medical procedure that aids a sibling. If the child is under such a duty, then so too are adults. Yet many would think it plausible to say that adults who act to save others by undergoing a medical procedure – which, however risk- and pain-free, has some costs – do something beyond the call of duty. Their action is supererogatory, not obligatory. Why, then, should it be any different with children?

The additional complication is that the child in the envisaged example does not act from her own volition. It is her parents who choose on her behalf. But if I am under a duty to do Ø then it is I who must discharge this duty, if I choose to do so, by doing Ø. The child does not choose to do what duty, allegedly, requires of her. Rather, the choice is made vicariously by others. Grant that parents do have a right to choose on behalf of their children – an idea challenged by the arguments of the previous chapter. It is still not clear that it makes sense to say that one person can choose whether, and in what manner, to discharge a duty that another is under.

Why, furthermore, would there not be an even more general problem of involuntary altruism (Elliott, 1998: 456–57)? Consider that there are things a child can do, or that can be done to a child, which produce good. These are things that a child may be said to be obliged to do, or have done to it, or which are supererogatory if done or endured by the child. Others may choose on behalf of the child so that these things are done. Not only the child's parents, but the state can vicariously choose for the child. Why, for instance, should not the state compel children to undergo paediatric research that is valuable not to them but to other children?

Certainly, there are limits to what may justifiably be done to a child in the name of medical good consequence. A distinction thus is normally drawn between therapeutic and non-therapeutic research, that is, between research that does and research that does not benefit the subject of that research. The problem of compelling children to undergo research – or at least of using them without their consent for such research – presses hardest when the research in question is non-therapeutic. Some who write on this topic insist that there must be a balance between the value of any such research and the abuse of paediatric subjects (Brody, 1998: 128–29). In general there is a presumption against using children for non-therapeutic research and a presumption to regard such use as permissible only when the risks to the children are negligible (Montgomery, 2001).

But why should children be used *at all*? Why is their use without their consent not properly regarded as a form of child *abuse*? The principles that should govern paediatric research are often cited as beneficence, respect for persons, and justice (Levine, 1996). Beneficence urges the maximization of possible benefits and the minimization of possible harms; respect for persons applies to our treatment of adults; and justice requires that we share the burdens and benefits of any course of action fairly. Why, then, should children who are not owed the respect that adults are owed be expected to bear the burdens of research that adults are not under any obligation to bear? Some do, indeed, take the view that using children without their consent is an unwarranted violation of the principle of respect for persons. Children cannot give their consent to such research, and no one else, such as the parents or the state, can give proxy consent on behalf of children. In these circumstances, their use in research without their consent does them fundamental moral wrong (Ramsey, 1970).

Perhaps it will be said that children are obliged to undergo paediatric research for the benefits of others because this is what they would agree to do if choosing, as adults, and fully apprised of the facts, the value of the research, and so on. Vicarious consent, on the child's behalf, might be described as morally permitted because such consent is 'a construction of what the child would wish could he consent for himself' and he would so choose 'if he were capable of choice because he *ought* to do so' (McCormick, 1974: 9). In the first place, it is a familiar criticism of hypothetical obligations that they do not obligate. As Ronald Dworkin has famously noted in another context with respect to contracts, 'a hypothetical contract is not simply a pale form of an actual contract; it is no contract at all' (Dworkin, 1975: 18). The fact that children would consent in specified hypothetical circumstances does not put them under the obligation that is assumed by their actually giving their consent.

Second, it is not clear why, if adults are not obligated to render the assistance in question, children would, as hypothetical adults, put themselves under such an obligation. Or, expressed the other way around, if hypothetical adults would put themselves under an obligation to help, why are actual adults not under that same obligation? Third, as we saw in the Chapter 1 discussion of 'best interests', it is by no means obvious, nor determinate, what a child would choose if she was an adult. I conclude that children are not obliged, either as family members or in general, to render assistance to others by undergoing medical procedures or being the subjects of medical research.

Summary

The state's interest in children consists in its being, as *parens patriae*, the protector of those within its jurisdiction who cannot protect themselves, and in the playing its reproductive role of ensuring the future viability and legitimacy of the polity. There are thus three sets of interests, or rights, to be balanced against one another – those of the state, those of the child and those of the parents.

The compulsory state education of children can be justified on weak paternalist grounds as being for the good of those who are not yet capable of deciding for themselves what is best. The complaint of parents that they do not approve of what the state teaches to their children is, in the final analysis, without warrant. For their part, children should be taught to make their own adult choices. The state has an interest in children receiving a civic education that prepares them for their role as adult citizens. It is arguable that such an education is the very same as one that creates autonomous adult individuals. Yet children also have interests in acquiring a certain kind of character and possibly in inheriting an identity that may be in tension with their interest in a maximally 'open future'.

Child protection (CP) practices are guided both by a concern for the child's best interests and by a concern to give due weight to the child's own views. The ideal of 'family integrity' that constrains the operation of CP practices decomposes into an ideal of familial privacy and a right of parental autonomy. The latter is, at most, only a discretion in the discharge of a duty to care for one's children. Parents do not, as parents, have rights over their children and thus are not in a position to make decisive claims as to the nature of any CP action in respect of the child. Familial privacy is an ideal but it should not, and need not, get in the way of the detection of serious harms to children.

Children are, as a rule, presumed incompetent to make medical decisions, but some can show themselves to be competent to do so. Nevertheless, all children ought to be consulted about medical procedures. The influence of parents upon their own children may vitiate the autonomy of the children. But, once again, parents' views on the care of their children should only be considered and given a certain weight if they are guided by a concern to promote the interests of the children.

Children are not obliged, even hypothetically, to undergo medical research for the benefit of their family members or for the benefit of people in general.

Note

1 What follows draws on Archard (2000).

Bibliography

Abrams, N. (1979), 'Problems in Defining Child Abuse and Neglect', in O. O'Neill and W. Ruddick (eds) (1979), pp. 156–63.

Aiken, W. and LaFollette, H. (eds) (1980), *Whose Child? Parental Rights, Parental Authority and State Power*, Totowa, NJ: Rowman and Littlefield.

Alderson, P. (1993), *Children's Consent to Surgery*, Buckingham: Open University Press.

Alston, P. (ed.) (1994), *The Best Interests of the Child: Reconciling Culture and Human Rights*, Oxford: Clarendon Press.

———, (1994), 'The Best Interests Principle: Towards a Reconciliation of Culture and Human Rights', in P. Alston (ed.) (1994), pp. 1–25.

Alston, P., Parker, S., and Seymour, J. (eds) (1992), *Children, Rights and the Law*, Oxford: Oxford University Press.

An-Na'im, A. (1994), 'Cultural Transformation and Normative Consensus on the Best Interests of the Child', in P. Alston (ed.) (1994), pp. 62–81.

Archard, D. (1993a), 'Self-justifying Paternalism', *The Journal of Value Inquiry*, 27, pp. 341–52.

———, (1993b), *Children, Rights and Childhood*, London: Routledge.

———, (1995), 'What's Blood Got to Do With It? The Significance of Natural Parenthood', *Res Publica*, 1(1): 91–106.

———, (1998), 'Can Child Abuse be Defined?', in M. King (ed.) *Moral Agendas for Children's Welfare*, London: Routledge: pp. 74–89.

———, (2000), *Sex Education*, Impact No. 7 Edit. by John White, London: Philosophy of Education Society of Great Britain.

Archard, D. and Macleod, C. (eds) (2002), *The Moral and Political Status of Children: New Essays*, Oxford: Oxford University Press.

Aristotle (1984), *Nichomachean Ethics*, trans. by W.D. Ross, rev. by J.O. Urmson, in J. Barnes (ed.), *The Complete Works of Aristotle*, Volume Two, Bollingen Series LXXI.2, Princeton, NJ: Princeton University Press.

Arneson, R.J. and Shapiro, I. (1996), 'Democratic Autonomy and Religious Freedom: A Critique of *Wisconsin* v. *Yoder*', in I. Shapiro and R. Hardin (eds), *Political Order*, Nomos XXXVIII, New York: New York University Press: pp. 365–411.

Barrie, J.M. (1995), *Peter Pan and Other Plays*, Edit. and intro. by Peter Hollindale, Oxford: Oxford University Press.

Barry, Brian (2001), *Culture and Equality, An Egalitarian Critique of Multiculturalism*, Oxford: Polity Press.

Beck, C.K., Glavis, G., Glover, S.A., Jenkins, M.B. and Nardi, R.A. (1978), 'The Rights of Children: A Trust Model', *Fordham Law Review*, **46**(4), pp. 669–780.

Becker, L.C. (1977), *Property Rights, Philosophic Foundations*, London: Routledge and Kegan Paul.

Behlmer, G.K. (1982), *Child Abuse and Moral Reform in England 1870–1908*, Stanford, CA: Stanford University Press.

Benatar, David (1997), 'Why It is Better Never to Come into Existence', *American Philosophical Quarterly*, **34**, pp. 345–55.

Bigelow, J., Campbell, J., Dodds, S.M., Pargetter, R., Prior, E.W. and Young, R. (1988), 'Parental Autonomy', *Journal of Applied Philosophy*, 5(2), pp. 183–96.

Blustein, J. (1982), *Parents and Children. The Ethics of the Family*, Oxford: Oxford University Press.

Boswell, J. (1988), *The Kindness of Strangers: The Abandonment of Children in Western Europe from Late Antiquity to the Renaissance*, New York: Random House.

Bourne, R. and Newberger, E.H. (1977), '"Family Autonomy" or "Coercive Intervention"? Ambiguity and Conflict in the Proposed Standards for Child Abuse and Neglect', *Boston University Law Review*, 57, pp. 670–76.

Brennan, S. and Noggle, R. (1997), 'The Moral Status of Children: Children's Rights, Parents' Rights, and Family Justice', *Social Theory and Practice*, **23**(1), pp. 1–26.

Brighouse, H. (1998), 'Civic Education and Liberal Legitimacy', *Ethics*, **108**(4), p. 719–45.

Brody, Baruch, A. (1998), *The Ethics of Biomedical Research. An International Perspective*, New York: Oxford University Press.

Brownlie, Ian (ed.) (1993), *Basic Documents on Human Rights*, Oxford: Oxford University Press.

Buchanan, Allen E. and Brock, Dan W. (1989), *Deciding for Others: The Ethics of Surrogate Decision Making*, Cambridge: Cambridge University Press.

Burley, Justine C. (1998), 'The Price of Eggs: Who Should Bear the Costs of Fertility Treatment?', in J. Harris and S. Holm (eds), *The Future of Human Reproduction: Ethics, Choice, and Regulation*, Oxford: Clarendon Press, pp. 127–49.

Burtt, S. (1996), 'In Defense of *Yoder*: Parental Authority and the Public Schools', in I. Shapiro and R. Hardin (eds), *Political Order*, Nomos XXXVIII, New York: New York University Press, pp. 412–37.

Callan, E. (1997), *Creating Citizens: Political Education and Liberal Democracy*, Oxford: Oxford University Press.

Campbell, T. (1992), 'The Rights of the Minor: as

Person, as Child, as Juvenile, as Future Adult', in P. Alston, S. Parker and J. Seymour (eds), *Children, Rights and the Law*, Oxford: Oxford University Press, pp. 1 -23.

Carter, R. (1977). 'Justifying Paternalism', *Canadian Journal of Philosophy* 7(1), pp. 133–45.

Casal, P. and Williams, A. (1995), 'Rights, Equality and Procreation', *Analyse & Kritik*, **17**, pp. 93–116.

Childress, James F. (1982), *Who Should Decide? Paternalism in Health Care*, New York: Oxford University Press.

Citizenship Advisory Group (1998), *Education for Citizenship and the Teaching of Democracy in Schools*, London: QCA.

Coady, C.A.J. (1992), 'Theory, Rights and Children: A Comment on O'Neill and Campbell', in P. Alston, S. Parker and J. Seymour (eds) (1992), pp. 43–51.

Cohen, G.A. (1989), 'On the Currency of Egalitarian Justice', *Ethics*, **99**, pp. 906–44.

———, (1995), *Self-ownership, freedom and equality*, Cambridge: Cambridge University Press.

———, (1997), 'Where the Action Is: On the Site of Distributive Justice', *Philosophy and Public Affairs*, **26**(1), pp. 3–30.

Cohen, H. (1980), *Equal Rights for Children*, Totowa, NJ: Littlefield, Adams & Co.

Cohen, J. (1992), 'Okin on Justice, Gender, and Family', *Canadian Journal of Philosophy*, **22**(2), pp. 263–86.

Coleman, J. (1998), 'Civic Pedagogies and Liberal-Democratic Curriculla', *Ethics*, **108**(4), pp. 746–61.

Craig, E. (ed.) (1998), *Routledge Encyclopedia of Philosophy*, London: Routledge.

Day, J.P. (1966), 'Locke on Property', *Philosophical Quarterly*, **16**, pp. 207–20.

Dent, G.W. (1988), 'Religious Children, Secular Schools', *Southern California Law Review*, **61**, pp. 886–93.

Dingwall, R., Eekelaar, J. and Murray, T. (1983), *The*

Protection of Children: State Intervention and Family Life, Oxford: Basil Blackwell.

Donzelot, J. (1980), *The Policing of Families: Welfare Versus the State*, trans. Robert Hurley, London: Hutchinson.

Dworkin, G. (1971), 'Paternalism', in R. Wasserstrom (ed.), *Morality and the Law*, Belmont, CA: Wadsworth, pp. 107–26.

Dworkin, R. (1975), 'The Original Position', in N. Daniels (ed.), *Reading Rawls: Critical Studies on Rawls's* A Theory of Justice, Oxford: Basil Blackwell, pp. 16–53.

———, (1977), *Taking Rights Seriously*, London: Duckworth.

Eekelaar, J. (1986a), 'The Eclipse of Parental Rights', *Law Quarterly Review*, **102**, pp. 4–9.

———, (1986b), 'The Emergence of Children's Rights', *Oxford Journal of Legal Studies*, 6, pp. 161–82.

Elliott, C. (1998), 'Patients Doubtfully Capable or Incapable of Consent', in H. Kuhse and P. Singer (eds), *A Companion to Bioethics*, Oxford: Basil Blackwell, pp. 452–62.

Elster, Jon (1989), *Solomonic Judgements, Studies in the Limitations of Rationality*, Cambridge: Cambridge University Press.

Exdell, J. (1994), 'Feminism, Fundamentalism, and Liberal Legitimacy', *Canadian Journal of Philosophy*, 24(3), pp. 441–64.

Farson, R. (1974), *Birthrights*, London: Collier Macmillan.

Feinberg, J. (1980), 'The Child's Right to an Open Future', in W. Aiken and H. LaFollette (eds) (1980), pp. 124–53.

Fishkin, J. (1983), *Justice, Equal Opportunity, and the Family*, New Haven, CT: Yale University Press.

Fried, C. (1978), *Right and Wrong*, Cambridge, MA: Harvard University Press.

Frisch, Lawrence E. (1981), 'On Licentious Licensing: A Reply to Hugh LaFollette', *Philosophy & Public Affairs*, **11**, pp. 173–80.

Galston, W. (1991), *Liberal Purposes: Goods, Virtues, and Diversity*, Cambridge: Cambridge University Press.

George, R. (1987), 'Who Should Bear the Cost of Children?', *Public Affairs Quarterly*, pp. 1–42.

———, (1994), 'On the External Benefits of Children', in D.T. Meyers, K. Kipnis and C.F. Murphy Jr. (eds), *Kindred Matters: Rethinking the Philosophy of the Family*, Ithaca: Cornell University Press, pp. 209–17.

Goldstein, J., Freud, A. and Solnit, J. (1973), *Beyond the Best Interests of the Child*, New York: Free Press.

———, (1979), *Before the Best Interests of the Child*, New York: Free Press.

Goodin, R. and Pettit, P. (eds) (1993), *A Companion to Contemporary Political Philosophy*, Oxford: Basil Blackwell.

Gordon, L. (2002), *Heroes of Their Own Lives: The Policies and History of Family Violence: Boston 1880–1960*, Chicago: University of Illinois Press.

Greenland, C. (1987), *Preventing CAN Deaths: An International Study of Deaths Due to Child Abuse and Neglect*, London: Tavistock.

Gutman, A. (1980), 'Children, Paternalism and Education: A Liberal Argument', *Philosophy and Public Affairs*, **9**(4), pp. 338–58.

———, (1985), 'Civic Education and Social Diversity', *Ethics*, **105**(3), pp. 557–79.

———, (1987), *Democratic Education*, Princeton, NJ: Princeton University Press.

Hall, B. (1999), 'The Origin of Parental Rights', *Public Affairs Quarterly*, **13**(1), pp. 73–82.

Halstead, J.M. (1997), 'Muslims and Sex Education', *Journal of Moral Education*, **26**(3), pp. 317–30.

Harding, Lorraine Fox (1991), *Perspectives in Child Care Policy*, London: Longman.

Harris, J. (1989), 'The Right to Found a Family', in G. Scarre (ed.), *Children, Parents and Politics*, Cambridge: Cambridge University Press, pp. 133–53.

Hart, H.L.A. (1973), 'Bentham on Legal Rights', in A.W. Simpson (ed.), *Oxford Essays in Jurisprudence*, Oxford: Oxford University Press, pp. 171–201.

Hobbes, Thomas (1994), *The Elements of Law, Natural and Politic* [1650], ed. and intro. by J.C.A. Gaskin, Oxford: Oxford University Press.

———, (1968) *Leviathan* [1651], ed. and intro. by C.B. Macpherson, Harmondsworth: Penguin.

Hobson, P. (1983), 'Paternalism and the Justification of Compulsory Education', *Australasian Journal of Education*, 27(2), pp. 136–50.

Holt, J. (1975), *Escape from Childhood: The Needs and Rights of Children*, Harmondsworth: Penguin.

Honneth, A. (1995), *The Struggle for Recognition: the Moral Grammar of Social Conflict*, trans. J. Anderson, Cambridge: Polity Press.

Houlgate, L. (ed.) (1998), *Family Values: Issues in Ethics, Society and the Family*, Boulder, Co.: Westview Press.

James, S. (1992), 'The Good-Enough Citizen: Female Citizenship and Independence', in G. Block and S. James (eds), *Beyond Equality and Difference*, London: Routledge, pp. 48–65.

Kant, I. (1963), *Lectures on Ethics*, trans. L. Infield, New York: Harper and Row.

———, (1996), *The Metaphysics of Morals*, trans. and ed. by Mary Gregor, intro. by Roger J. Sullivan, Cambridge: Cambridge University Press.

Kilbrandon, Lord (1995), *The Kilbrandon Report: Children and Young Persons, Scotland*, 3rd edn, London: The Stationery Office Books.

Kopelman, L.M. (1997a), 'Children and Bioethics:

Uses and Abuses of the Best-Interests Standard', *The Journal of Medicine and Philosophy*, 22, pp. 213–17.

———, (1997b), 'The Best-Interests Standard as Threshold, Ideal, and Standard of Reasonableness', *The Journal of Medicine and Philosophy*, 22, pp. 271–89.

Kramer, M.H., Simmonds, N.E., and Steiner, H. (1998), *A Debate Over Rights, Philosophical Enquiries*, Oxford: Clarendon Press.

Kramer, M.H. (1998), 'Rights Without Trimmings', in M. Kramer, N.E. Simmonds and H. Steiner (1998), pp. 7–111.

Kuhse, H. and Singer, P. (eds) (1998), *A Companion to Bioethics*, Oxford: Basil Blackwell.

Kymlicka, W. (1989), *Liberalism, Community and Culture*, Oxford: Clarendon Press.

———, (2002), *Contemporary Political Philosophy, An Introduction*, 2nd edn, Oxford: Oxford University Press.

Lacey, W.K. (1986), '*Patria potestas*', in B. Rawsin (ed.), *The Family in Ancient Rome: New Perspectives*, London: Croom Helm, pp. 120–44.

Ladd, Rosalind Ekman (ed.) (1996), *Children's Rights Re-Visioned: Philosophical Readings*, Belmont: Wadsworth Publishing Company.

LaFollette, H, (1980), 'Licensing Parents', *Philosophy and Public Affairs*, 9(2), pp. 182–97.

———, (1989) 'Freedom of Religion and Children', *Public Affairs Quarterly*, 3, pp. 75–87.

———, (1993), 'Personal Relationships', in P. Singer (ed.), *A Companion to Ethics*, Oxford: Basil Blackwell, pp. 327–32.

Laing, R.D. (1960), *The Divided Self*, Harmondsworth: Penguin.

———, (1967). *The Politics of Experience*, Harmondsworth: Penguin.

Larkin, P. (1988), *Collected Poems*, ed. and intro. by

Anthony Thwaite, London: The Marvell Press and Faber and Faber.

Lasch, C. (1977), *Haven in a Heartless World: The Family Besieged*, New York: Basic Books.

Laslett, P. (1963), *The World We Have Lost*, London: Methuen.

Leach, E. (1968), *A Runaway World? Reith Lectures 1967*, Oxford: Oxford University Press.

LeBlanc, Lawrence J. (1995), *The Convention on the Rights of the Child. United Nations Lawmaking on Human Rights*, Lincoln: University of Nebraska Press.

Levine, R.J. (1996), 'Research involving children as subjects', in D.C. Thomasman and T. Kushner (eds), *Birth to Death: Science and Bioethics*, Cambridge: Cambridge University Press, pp. 270–82.

Liao, S.M. (2000), The Right of Children to be Loved, DPhil thesis, University of Oxford, Michaelmas.

Lloyd, S.A. (1994), 'Family Justice and Social Justice', *Pacific Philosophical Quarterly*, 75, pp. 353–71.

Locke, J. (1961), *An Essay Concerning Human Understanding* [1689], ed. J. Yolton, London: Dent.

———, (1960), *Some Thoughts Concerning Education* [1693], in *The Educational Writings of John Locke*, ed. J.L. Axtell, Cambridge: Cambridge University Press.

———, (1963), *Two Treatises of Government* [1698], A critical edition with an Introduction and *apparatus criticus* by Peter Laslett, Cambridge: Cambridge University Press.

Lockyer, A. and Stone, F.H. (eds) (1998), *Juvenile Justice in Scotland: Twenty-Five Years of the Welfare Approach*, London: Butterworths.

MacCormick, N. (1976), 'Children's Rights: A Test-Case for Theories of Rights', *Archiv für Rechts und Sozialphilosophie*, 62(3), pp. 305–17; reprinted in his *Legal Right and Social Democracy: Essays in Legal and Political Philosophy*, Oxford: Clarendon Press (1982), pp. 154–66.

Macedo, S. (1995), 'Liberal Civic Education and Religious Fundamentalism', *Ethics*, **105**(3), pp. 468–96.

MacKenzie, Lord (1862), *Studies in Roman Law*, Edinburgh: William Blackwood & Sons.

Macleod, C.M. (1997), 'Conceptions of Parental Autonomy', *Politics and Society*, **25**(1), pp. 117–40.

———, (2002), 'Liberal Equality and the Affective Family', in D. Archard and C. Macleod (eds) (2002), pp. 212–23.

Mahall, B. (1995), 'The Changing Context of Childhood: Children's Perspectives on Health Care Resources Including Services', in B. Botting (ed.), *The Health of our Children*, decennial supplement, Office of Population, Censuses and Surveys, London: HMSO, pp. 21–7.

Mahowald, M.B. (1996), 'On caring for children', in D.C. Thomasman and T. Kushner (eds), *Birth to Death: Science and Bioethics*, Cambridge: Cambridge University Press, pp. 85–98.

Margalit, A. and Raz, J. (1995), 'National Self-Determination', in W. Kymlicka (ed.), *The Rights of Minority Cultures*, Oxford: Oxford University Press, pp. 79–92. Originally published in *Journal of Philosophy*, 87(9) (1990), pp. 439–61.

Mause, L. de (1976), 'The Evolution of Childhood', in de Mause, *The History of Childhood*, London: Souvenir Press, pp. 1–73.

McCormick, Richard A. (1974), 'Proxy Consent in Experimentation Situations', *Perspectives in Biology and Medicine*, **18**, pp. 2–20.

McGough, Lucy S. (1995), 'Children: V Child Custody', in *Encyclopedia of Bioethics*, rev. edn. Warren T. Reich, New York: Simon & Schuster Macmillan, pp. 371–78.

McKay, A. (1997), 'Accommodating Ideological Pluralism in Sexuality Education', *Journal of Moral Education*, **26**(3), pp. 285–300.

Meyers, Diania Tietjens, Kipnis, Kenneth and Murphy, Cornelius F. Jr. (eds) (1993), *Kindred Matters: Rethinking the Philosophy of the Family*, Ithaca, NY: Cornell University Press.

Mill, J.S. (1984), *The Subjection of Women* [1869], in J.M. Robson (ed.), *Collected Works of John Stuart Mill*, Volume XXI: *Essays on Equality, Law, and Education*, Toronto: Toronto University Press.

Mnookin, Robert H. (1979), 'Foster Care – In Whose Best Interests?', in O. O'Neill and W. Ruddick (eds) (1979), pp. 179–213.

Montague, P. (2000), 'The Myth of Parental Rights', *Social Theory and Practice*, **26**(1), pp. 47–68.

Montgomery, Jonathan (1988), 'Children as Property?', *The Modern Law Review*, **51**, pp. 323–42.

———, (2001), 'Informed Consent and Clinical Research with Children', in L. Doyal and J.S. Tobias (eds), *Informed Consent in Medical Research*, London: BMJ Books, pp. 173–81.

Munoz-Dardé, V. (1998), 'Rawls, Justice in the Family and Justice of the Family', *Philosophical Quarterly*, **48**, pp. 335–52.

———, (1999), 'Is the Family to be Abolished Then?', *Proceedings of the Aristotelian Society*, **99**, pp. 37–56.

Murray, Thomas H. (1996), *The Worth of a Child*, Berkeley: University of California Press.

Narayan, U. and Bartowiak, Julia J. (eds) (1999), *Having and Raising Children: Unconventional families, Hard Choices and the Social Good*, University Park, Pennsylvania: Pennsylvania State University Press.

Narveson, J. (1998), *The Libertarian Idea*, Philadelphia: Temple University Press.

Nelson, Hilde Lindemann (ed.) (1997), *Feminism and Families*, London: Routledge.

Nelson, Hilde Lindemann and Nelson, James Lindemann (1995), *The patient in the family: an ethics of medicine and families*, New York: Routledge.

Nicholas, B. (1962), *An Introduction to Roman Law*, Oxford: Clarendon Press.

Nozick, R. (1974), *Anarchy, State, and Utopia*, Oxford: Basil Blackwell.

———, (1989), *The Examined Life: Philosophical Meditations*, New York: Simon & Schuster.

Okin, S.M. (1982), 'Women and the Making of the Sentimental Family', *Philosophy & Public Affairs*, **11**, pp. 65–88.

———, (1989), *Justice, Gender, and the Family*, New York: Basic Books.

———, (1994), '*Political Liberalism*, Justice, and Gender', *Ethics*, **105**, pp. 23–43.

Olsen, Frances E. (1985), 'The Myth of State Intervention in the Family', *University of Michigan Journal of Law Reform*, **18**, pp. 835–64.

O'Neill, O. (1988), 'Children's Rights and Children's Lives', *Ethics*, **98**, pp. 445–63. Reprinted in P. Alston, S. Parker and J. Seymour (eds) (1992), pp. 24–42.

O'Neill, O. and Ruddick, W. (eds) (1979), *Having Children: Philosophical and Legal Reflections on Parenthood*, Oxford: Oxford University Press.

Page, E. (1984), 'Parental Rights', *Journal of Applied Philosophy*, **1**(2), pp. 187–203.

Parfit, D. (1984), *Reasons and Persons*, Oxford: Oxford University Press.

Parker, S. (1994), 'The Best Interests of the Child – Principles and Problems', in P. Alston (ed.) (1994), pp. 26–41.

Pateman, C. (1987), 'Feminist Critiques of the Public/Private Dichotomy', in A. Phillips (ed.), *Feminism and Equality*, Oxford: Blackwell, pp. 103–26.

Plato (1941), *The Republic*, trans. Francis Cornford, Oxford: Oxford University Press.

Pollock, L. (1983), *Forgotten Children: Parent-Child Relations from 1500 to 1900*, Cambridge: Cambridge University Press.

Purdy, L.M. (1992), *In Their Best Interest? The Case Against Equal Rights for Children*, Ithaca, NY and London: Cornell University Press.

Ramsey, P. (1970), *The Patient as Person*, New Haven, CT: Yale University Press.

Rawls, J. (1972), *A Theory of Justice*, Oxford: Oxford University Press.

———, (1993), *Political Liberalism*, New York: Columbia University Press.

Raz, J. (1984), 'Legal Rights', *Oxford Journal of Legal Studies*, **4**(1), pp. 1–21.

Reiss, M.J. and Mabud, S.A. (eds) (1998), *Sex Education and Religion*, Cambridge: The Islamic Academy.

Robertson, J. (1983), 'Procreative Liberty and the Control of Conception, Pregnancy and Childbirth', *Virginia Law Review*, **69**, pp. 405–64.

Roemer, J. (1999), 'Egalitarian Strategies', *Dissent*, **46**(3), pp. 64–74.

Rousseau, Jean-Jacques (1991), *Émile or On Education*, trans. with an introduction and notes by Allan Bloom, Harmondsworth: Penguin.

Russell, J.S. (1995), 'Okin's Rawlsian Feminism? Justice in the Family and Another Liberalism', *Social Theory and Practice*, **21**(3), Fall, pp. 397–426.

Sandel, M. (1982), *Liberalism and the Limits of Justice*, Cambridge: Cambridge University Press.

Scarre, G. (ed.) (1989), *Children, Parents and Politics*, Cambridge: Cambridge University Press.

Schoeman, F. (1980), 'Rights of Families: Rights of Parents, and the Moral Basis of The Family', *Ethics*, **91**, pp. 6–19.

Schrag, F. (1980), 'Children: Their Rights and Needs', in W. Aiken and H. LaFollette (eds) (1980), pp. 237–53.

Singer, P. and Wells, D. (1984), *The Reproduction Revolution: New Ways of Making Babies*, Oxford: Oxford University Press.

Smart, Carol (1982), 'Regulating Families or

Legitimating Patriarchy? Family Law in Britain', *International Journal of the Sociology of Law*, **10**, pp. 129–47.

Steiner, H. (1994), *An Essay on Rights*, Oxford: Blackwell.

———, (1998), 'Working Rights', in M.H. Kramer, N.E. Simmonds and H. Steiner (1998).

Stone, L. (1977), *The Family, Sex and Marriage in England 1500–1800*, London: Wiedenfeld & Nicolson.

Sugarman, J. *et al* (1999), 'Empirical Research on Informed Consent. An Annotated Bibliography', *Hastings Center Report*, **29**, Special Supplement, pp. S1–S42.

Sumner, L.W. (1987), *The Moral Foundation of Rights*, Oxford: Clarendon Press.

Taylor, C. (1985), 'The Nature and Scope of Distributive Justice', in C. Taylor, *Philosophy and the Human Sciences, Philosophical Papers*, Vol. 2, Cambridge: Cambridge University Press, pp. 289–317.

Tolstoy, L. (1954), *Anna Karenin*, trans. and intro. Rosemary Edmonds, Harmondsworth: Penguin.

Turner, Susan M. and Matthews, Gareth B. (eds) (1998), *The Philosopher's Child: Critical Perspectives in the Western Tradition*, Rochester: University of Rochester Press.

Ulanowsky, C. (ed.) (1995), *The Family in the Age of Technology*, Aldershot: Avebury.

United Nations (1989), *The Convention on the Rights of the Child*, reprinted in P. Alston, S. Parker and J. Seymour (eds) (1992), pp. 245–64.

UNICEF (United Nations Children's Fund) (2000), *The State of the World's Children*, Geneva: UNICEF.

Vallentyne, P. (2002), 'Equality and the Duties of Procreators', in D. Archard and C. Macleod (eds) (2002), pp. 195–211.

Vallentyne, P. and Lipson, M. (1989), 'Equal Opportunity and the Family', *Public Affairs Quarterly*, 3(4), pp. 39–45.

Wald, Michael (1975), 'State Intervention on Behalf of "Neglected" Children: A Search for Realistic Standards', *Stanford Law Review*, **27**, pp. 985–1040.

Waldfogel, J. (1998), *The Future of Child Protection – How to Break the Cycle of Abuse and Neglect*, Cambridge, Mass.: Harvard University Press.

Walzer, M. (1983), *Spheres of Justice. A Defence of Pluralism and Equality*, Oxford: Basil Blackwell.

White, P. (1991), 'Parents' rights, homosexuality and education', *British Journal of Educational Studies*, **39**(4), pp. 398–408.

Wijze, S. de (1999), 'Rawls and Civic Education', *Cogito*, **13**(2), pp. 87–93.

Williams, G. (1985), 'The Gillick Saga – II' *New Law Journal*, 29, pp. 1179–82.

Wong, D. (1998), 'Relativism', in P. Singer (ed.), *A Companion to Ethics*, Oxford: Basil Blackwell, pp. 442–50.

Young, Robert (1998), 'Informed Consent and Patient Autonomy', in H. Kuhse and P. Singer (eds), (1998), *A Companion to Bioethics*, Oxford: Basil Blackwell.

List of Legal Cases

Gillick v *West Norfolk and Wisbech Area Health Authority* [1986] AC 112.
Mozert v *Hawkins County Public School* [1987] 827 F 2d 1058, 102 ALR Fed 497.
Pierce v *Society of Sisters* [1925] 69 L Ed 1070.
Prince v *Commonwealth of Massachusetts* [1944] 99 L Ed 645.
Re W (a minor) [1992] 4 All ER 627.
Wisconsin v *Yoder* [1972] 32 L Ed 2d 15.

Index